Dear Student,

The code below gives you access to the user's area at the **StandFor Digital website**. There, you'll find a variety of multimedia content to make your learning experience more interactive.

Register at **digital.standfor.com.br** and activate the code to start using all the resources that accompany your course book. You can also download your interactive digital book.

M2F9NxJQ

With **StandFor Digital** all the resources you need are just a click away!

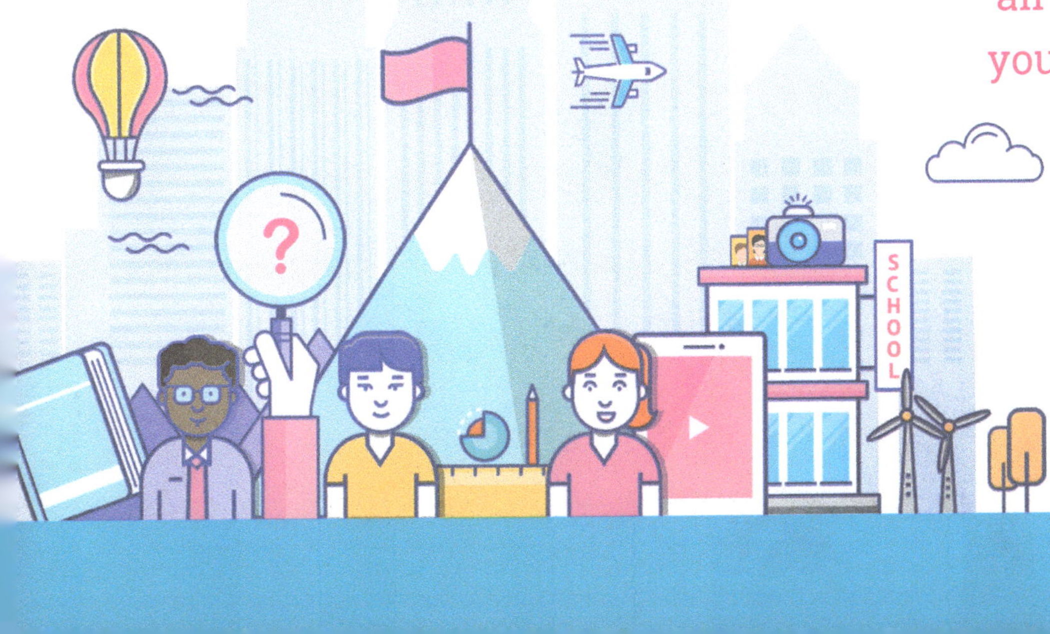

POP

CONTENTS

WELCOME 4
UNIT 1 A, B, C 6
UNIT 2 FAMILY PICTURE 14
REVIEW 1 AND 2 22

UNIT 3 LOOKS 24
UNIT 4 WILD ANIMALS 32
REVIEW 3 AND 4 40

UNIT 5 HOW MANY? 42
UNIT 6 MY ROUTINE 50
REVIEW 5 AND 6 58

UNIT 7 PLACES AROUND 60
UNIT 8 YUMMY! 68
REVIEW 7 AND 8 76

EXTRAS
GLOSSARY 78
WORKBOOK 80
BOOK INSTRUCTIONS 112
STICKERS 114

CLASSROOM LANGUAGE

What does "airplane" mean?

How do you say "avião" in English?

Sorry, I don't understand.

I'm done!

Can you repeat that?

Can I ask a question?

Can I get some water?

WELCOME!

1 Play the game! AUDIO TRACK 2

Hi, I'm Lily!

Hello! I'm Alex!

Welcome to POP 3. Let's have fun!

The mother of your mother.
Your Grandma.

The number between 5 and 7.
Six (6).

A name of a fruit with letter "o".

Orange.

The animal that flies in the sky.

Bird.

A toy with letter "b".

Ball/Building blocks.

The body part that you use to see.

Eyes.

The room where you sleep.

Bedroom.

The number between 13 and 15.

Fourteen (14).

LESSON 2

1 Listen and say. AUDIO TRACK 5

A B C D E
F G H I J K
L M N O P
Q R S T U V
W X Y Z

2 Look and write.

Vowels	Consonants
	B ___ D F ___ H J ___
A ___ I ___ U	___ M N ___ Q R ___
	___ V ___ X ___ Z

 **3** Stick in alphabetical order. STICK 114

 **4** Play Hangman. 81

Letters

LESSON 3

1 Look. Ask and write.

Can you spell your last name?	
Classmate	**Last name**

2 Look and complete.

bear ◆ game

a. teddy _____

b. video _____

3 Look and write. WORKBOOK 82

a. L O L D _____
b. R A C _____
c. L A L B _____
d. L A Y D U G O H P _____

OUR VALUES

Draw and color.

LESSON 4

1 Listen. Read and circle. AUDIO TRACK 6

a. The girl's name is …
   ☐ Judy.
   ☐ Julia.

b. They are …
   ☐ at home.
   ☐ at school.

2 Complete the comic strip.

spell ◆ can ◆ you ◆ love

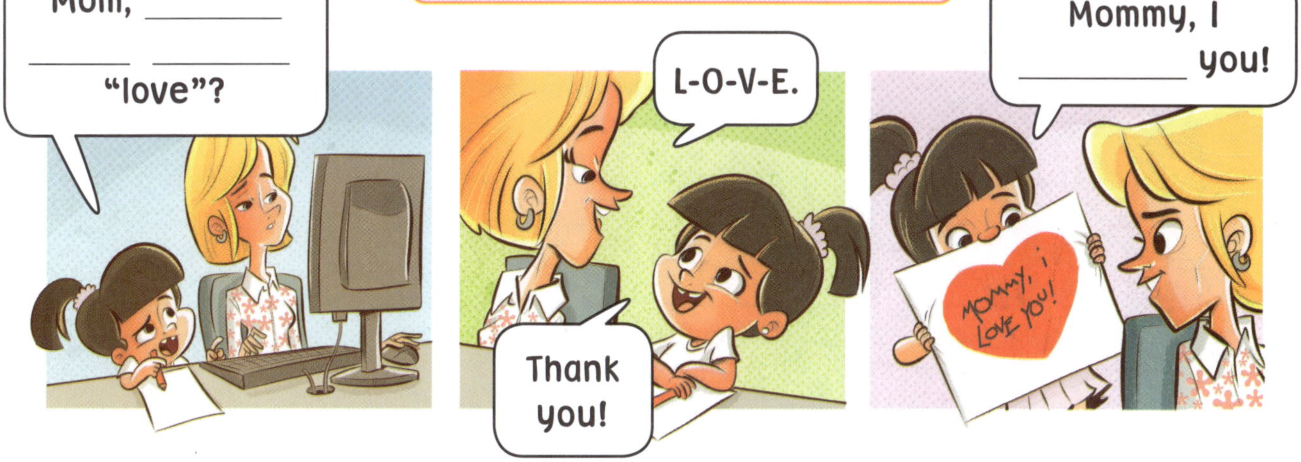

Mom, _____ _____ "love"?

L-O-V-E.

Thank you!

Mommy, I _____ you!

3 Look. Ask and answer. WORKBOOK 83

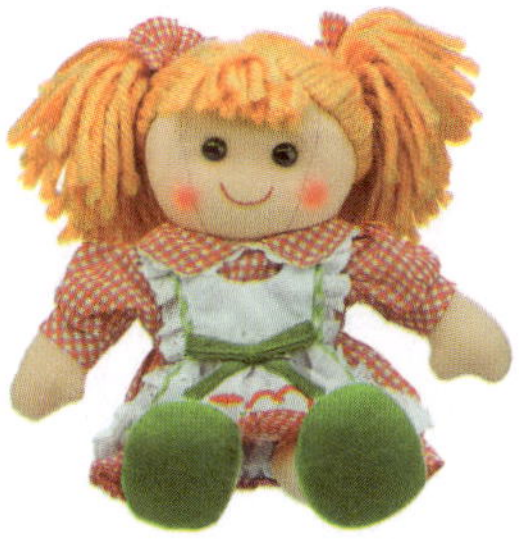

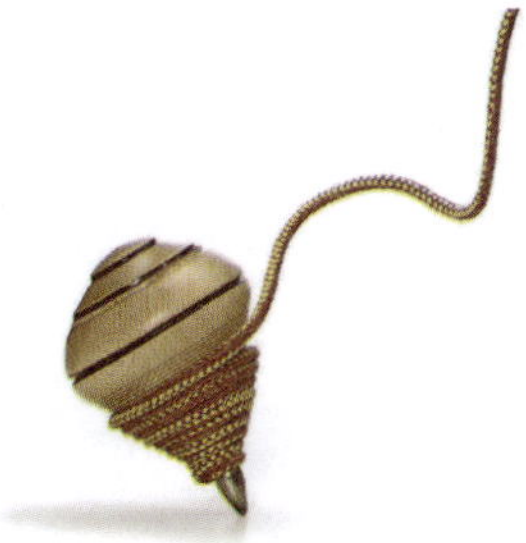

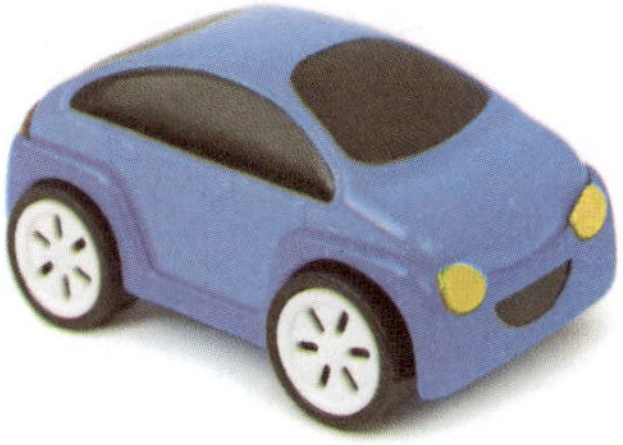

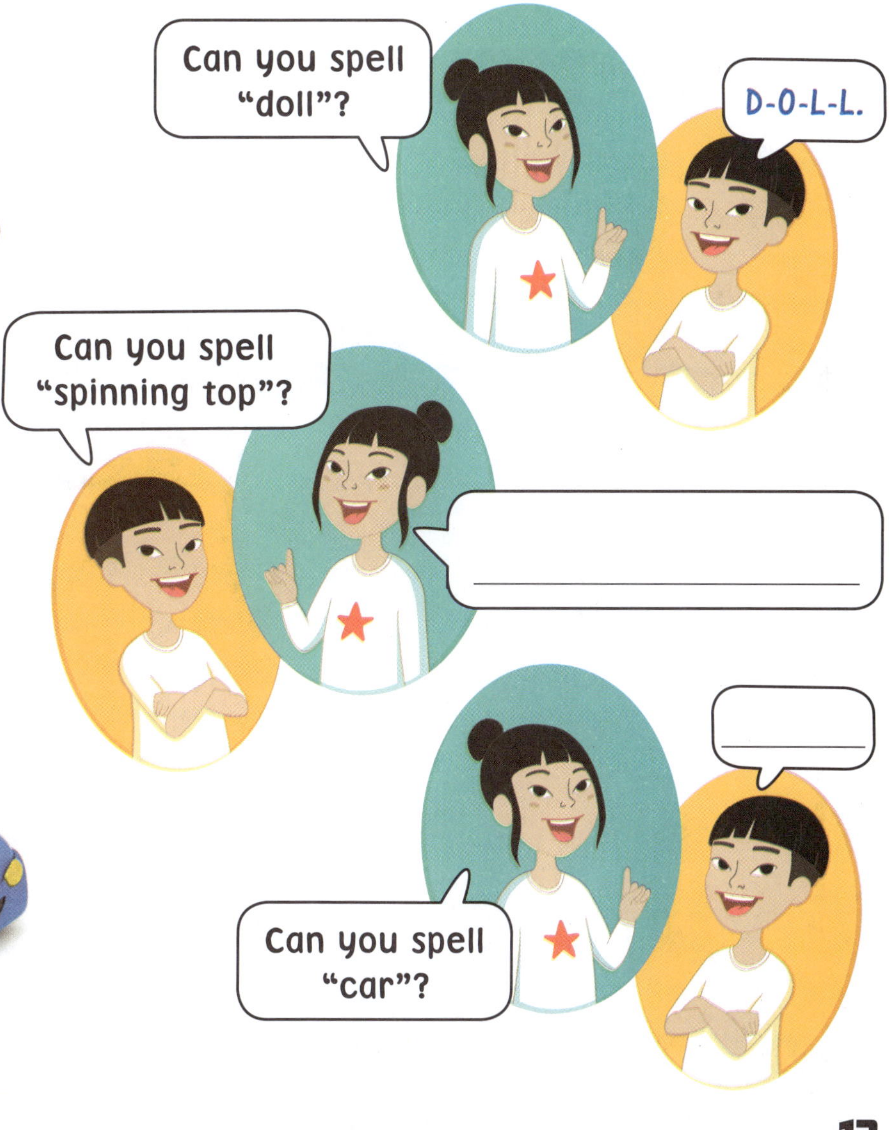

Can you spell "doll"?

D-O-L-L.

Can you spell "spinning top"?

_____

Can you spell "car"?

_____

UNIT 2

FAMILY PICTURE

LESSON 1

1 Look and listen. AUDIO TRACK 7

LESSON 2

1 Look. Read and stick. STICK 114

HALEY'S FAMILY TREE

TOM — MARY — STAN — SILVIA

LILIAN — PAUL — PETER — CINDY

CAROL — HANNAH — CHRIS — HALEY — DAVID

16

2 Read and complete.

Haley's Family

a. Hannah is Cindy's _____
b. Cindy is Carol's _____.
c. Lilian is Chris's _____.
d. David is Carol's _____.
e. Peter is Hannah's _____.
f. Chris is Paul's _____.

3 Circle and listen.

a. Haley is Cindy and Peter's **daughter** / **niece** / **son**.

b. Lilian and Paul's daughters are **Carol and Hannah** / **Chris and David** / **Hannah and Haley**.

c. Tom and Mary have two **daughters** / **sons**.

d. Stan and Silvia have **one** / **two** / **three** daughter(s).

LESSON 3

1 Look and write.

PAST

PRESENT

a. Who can you see in the old picture?

_____

b. Who can you see in the modern picture?

_____

2 Draw and color. Write. WORKBOOK 86

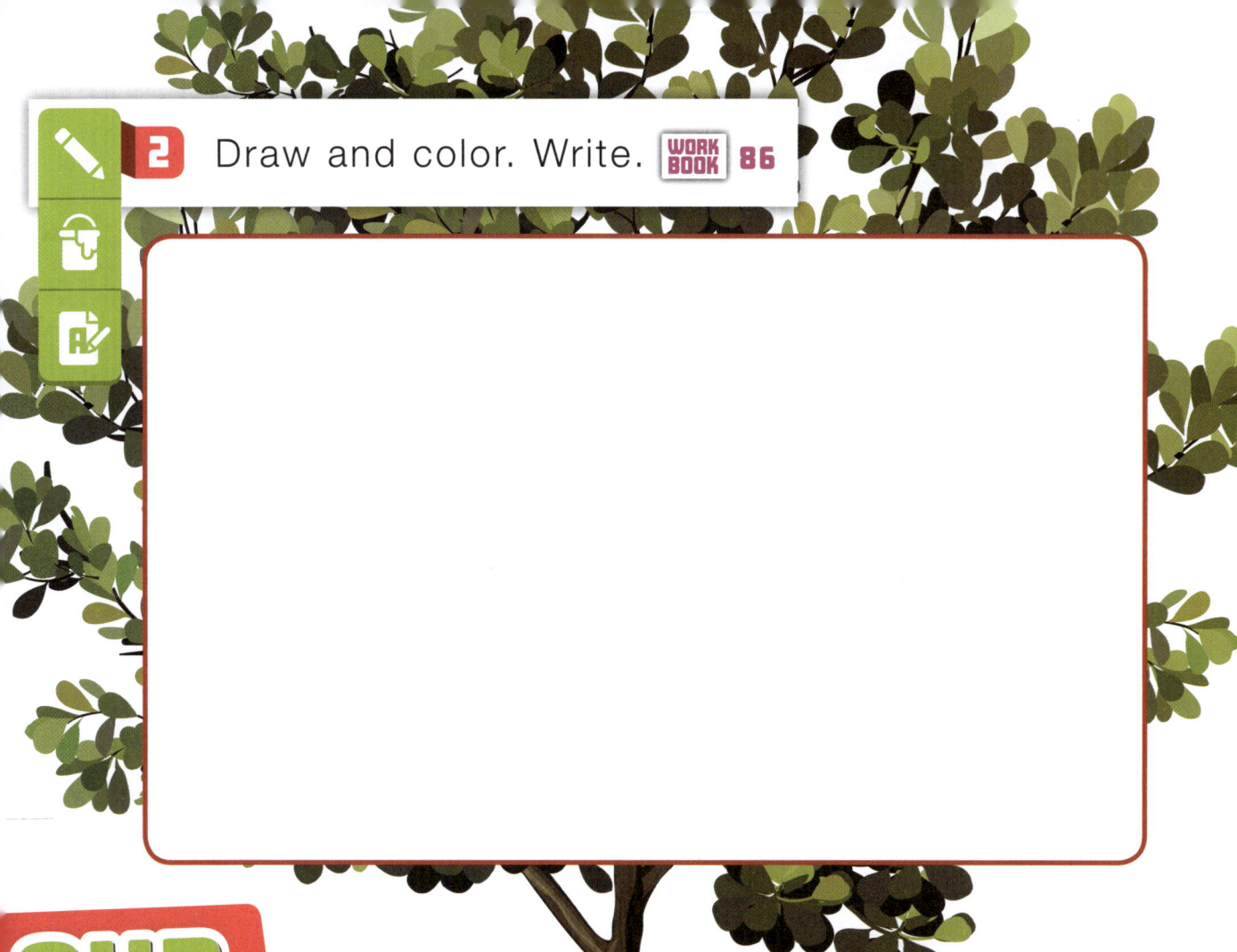

OUR VALUES

Color.

LESSON 4

1 Listen. Read and write. 10

a. What's the mom's name? _____
b. What's the dad's name? _____
c. What is the grandpa's name? _____
d. What's the daughter's name? _____
e. What's the grandma's name? _____

2 Draw and write. WORK BOOK 87

FOLLOW

I'm ______________________ (name). I have

a ______________________ (big / small) family.

My ______________________'s name

is ______________________ and my

____.

I love ______________________.

REVIEW 1·2

1 Look at the code and write the words.

A	B	C	D	E	F	G	H	I	J
1	2	3	4	5	6	7	8	9	10
K	L	M	N	O	P	Q	R	S	T
11	12	13	14	15	16	17	18	19	20
	U	V	W	X	Y	Z			
	21	22	23	24	25	26			

a. 4 – 15 – 12 – 12 = doll

b. _____

c. _____

d. _____

e. _____

f. _____

g. _____

2 Listen. Write and match. 🎧 11

a. _____

b. _____

c. _____

d. _____

3 Read the clues and write the words in the crossword puzzle.

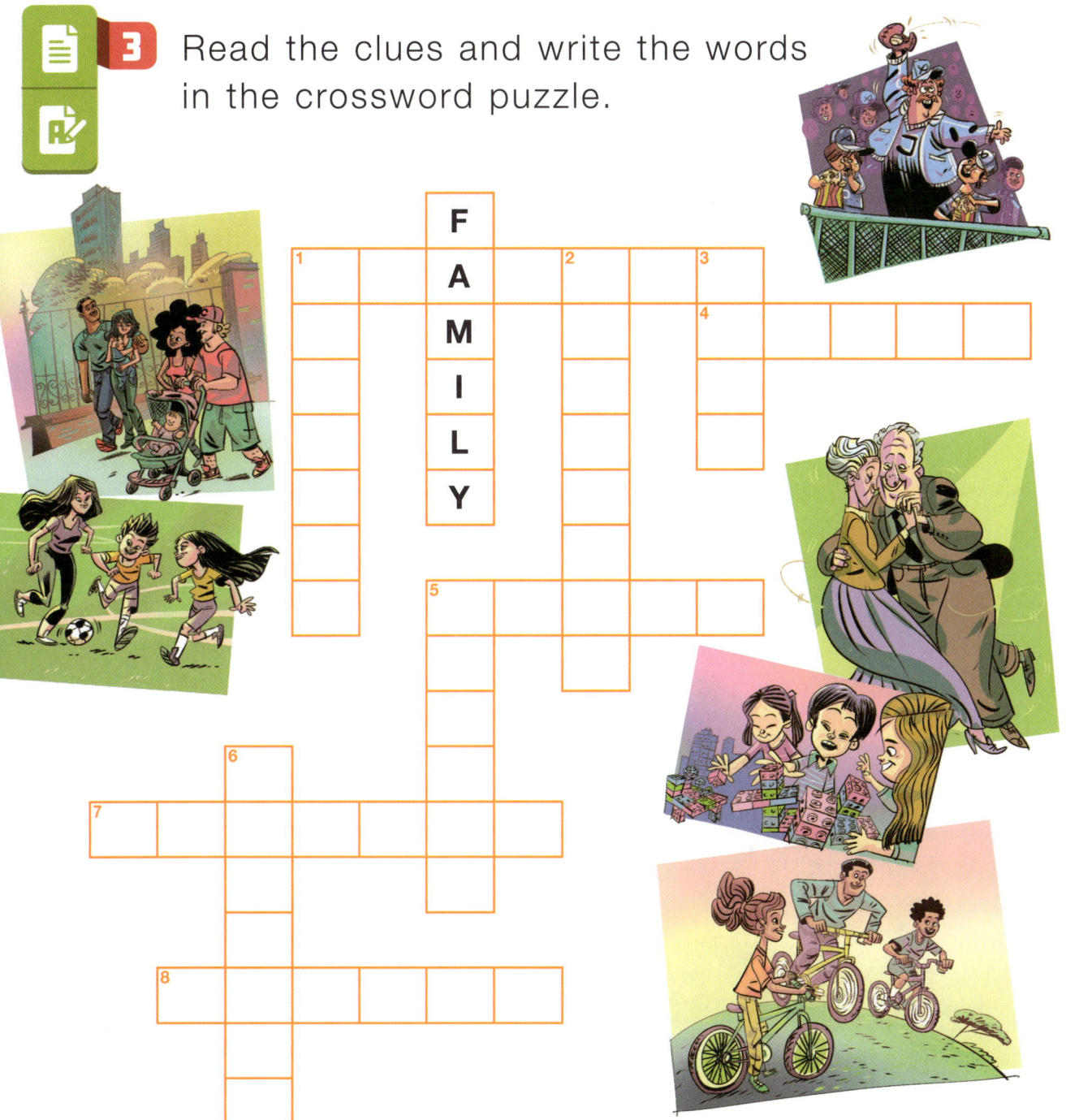

ACROSS →
1. My dad's mom.
4. My mom's brother.
5. My sister's daughter.
7. My mom's son.
8. My dad's daughter.

DOWN ↓
1. My dad's dad.
2. My sister is my mom's…
3. My dad's sister.
5. My brother's son.
6. My uncle's son and daughter.

UNIT 3
LOOKS
LESSON 1

1 Look. Listen and point. AUDIO TRACK 12

DORA

CHLOE

ALICE

LESSON 2

1 Look and read. Write.

a. I have green eyes. ☐

b. I have blond hair. ☐

c. I have brown hair. ☐

d. I have brown eyes. ☐

e. I have black hair. ☐

f. I have blue eyes. ☐

2 Read and complete. WORKBOOK 89

a. I _____ brown eyes. My mom _____ brown eyes too.

b. My dad _____ red hair, and I _____ red hair too.

c. My grandma _____ gray hair, but I _____ brown hair.

d. My mom _____ long hair, but I _____ short hair.

3 Look and match.

LESSON 3

1 Listen and match. AUDIO TRACK 14

a. He has blue eyes and blond hair.
b. She has green eyes.
c. She has brown eyes and brown hair.
d. He has gray hair and blue eyes.
e. She has red hair.
f. She has gray hair.

2 Listen and complete. AUDIO TRACK 15

a.

b.

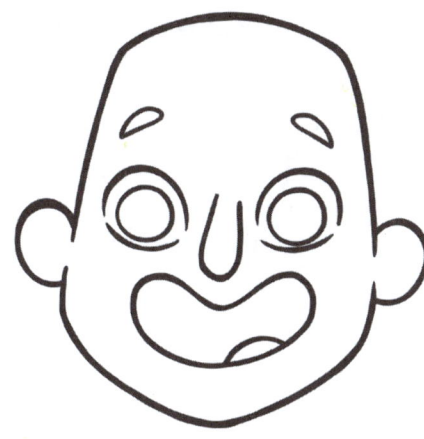

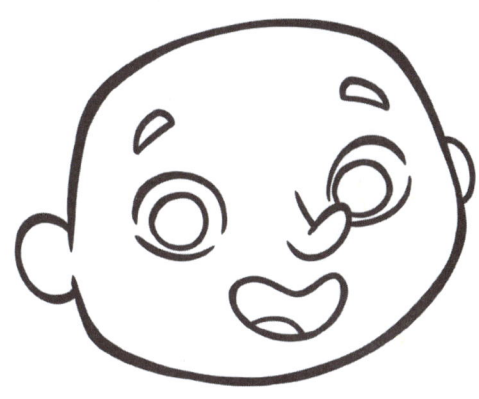

OUR VALUES

WORK BOOK 90

Color.

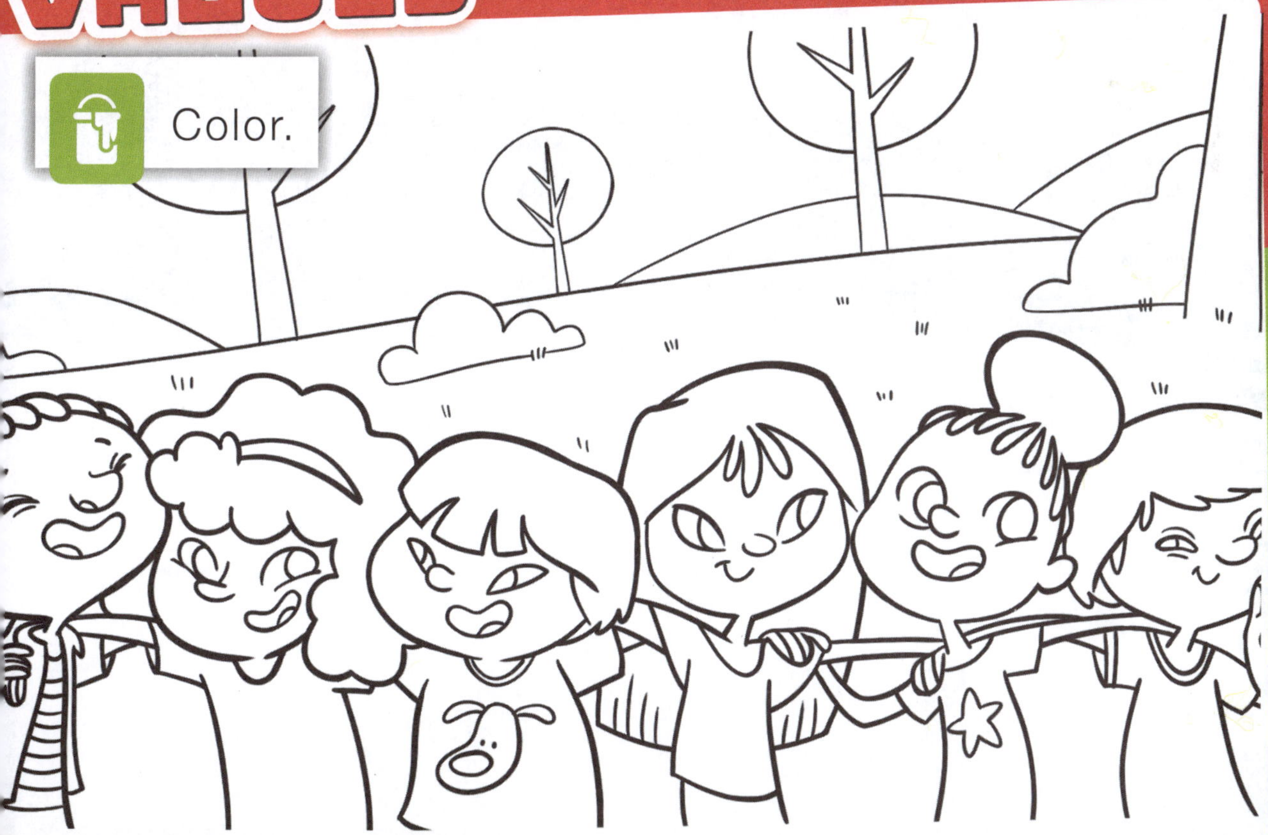

LESSON 4

 Read and write the answers.

Miles Morales

Name: Miles Morales

Gender: male

Age: 16 years old

Occupation: student, adventurer, vigilante

Hometown: Brooklyn, New York City

Hair: short and black

Eyes: brown

Species: human mutate

Family: Jefferson Davis (father)

Rio Morales (mother)

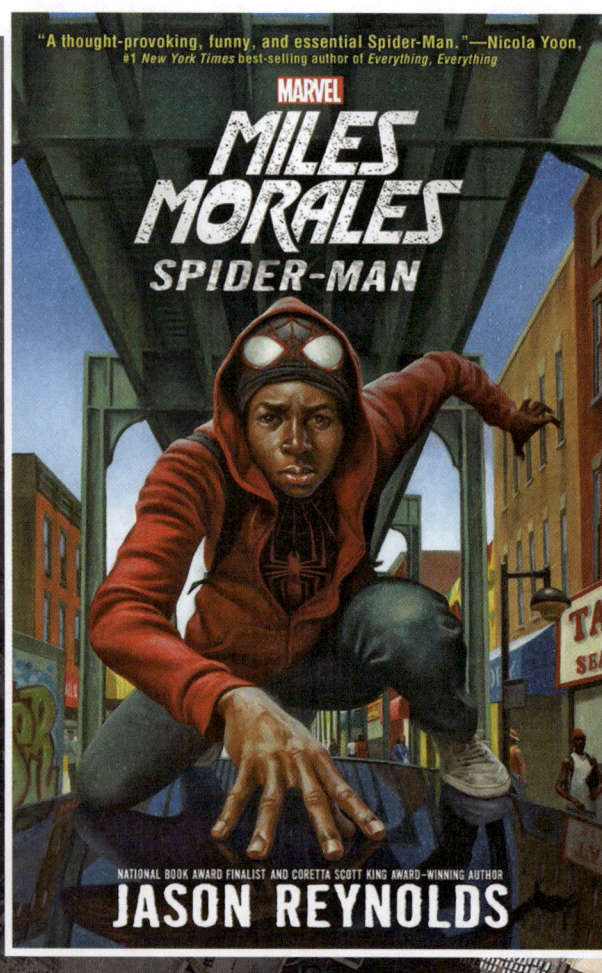

Source: <https://marvel.fandom.com/wiki/Miles_Morales_(Earth-1610)>. Accessed Feb. 20, 2019.

a. What is the name of the character?

b. What color are Miles Morales' eyes?

c. What color is Miles Morales' hair?

2 Look. Read and write to complete the text.

Princess Merida of DunBroch

Name: Merida.
Gender: female.
Age: 16 years old.
Occupation: _____.
Home: Scotland.
Hair: _____.
Eyes: _____.
Species: _____.
Family: King Fergus (_____.)
Queen Elinor (_____.)
Princes Harris, Hubert, and Hamish (_____.)

Source: <https://en.wikipedia.org/wiki/Merida_(Disney)>. Accessed Feb. 20, 2019.

3 Read and write your answer.

Who's your favorite fictional character?
My favorite fictional character is _____.

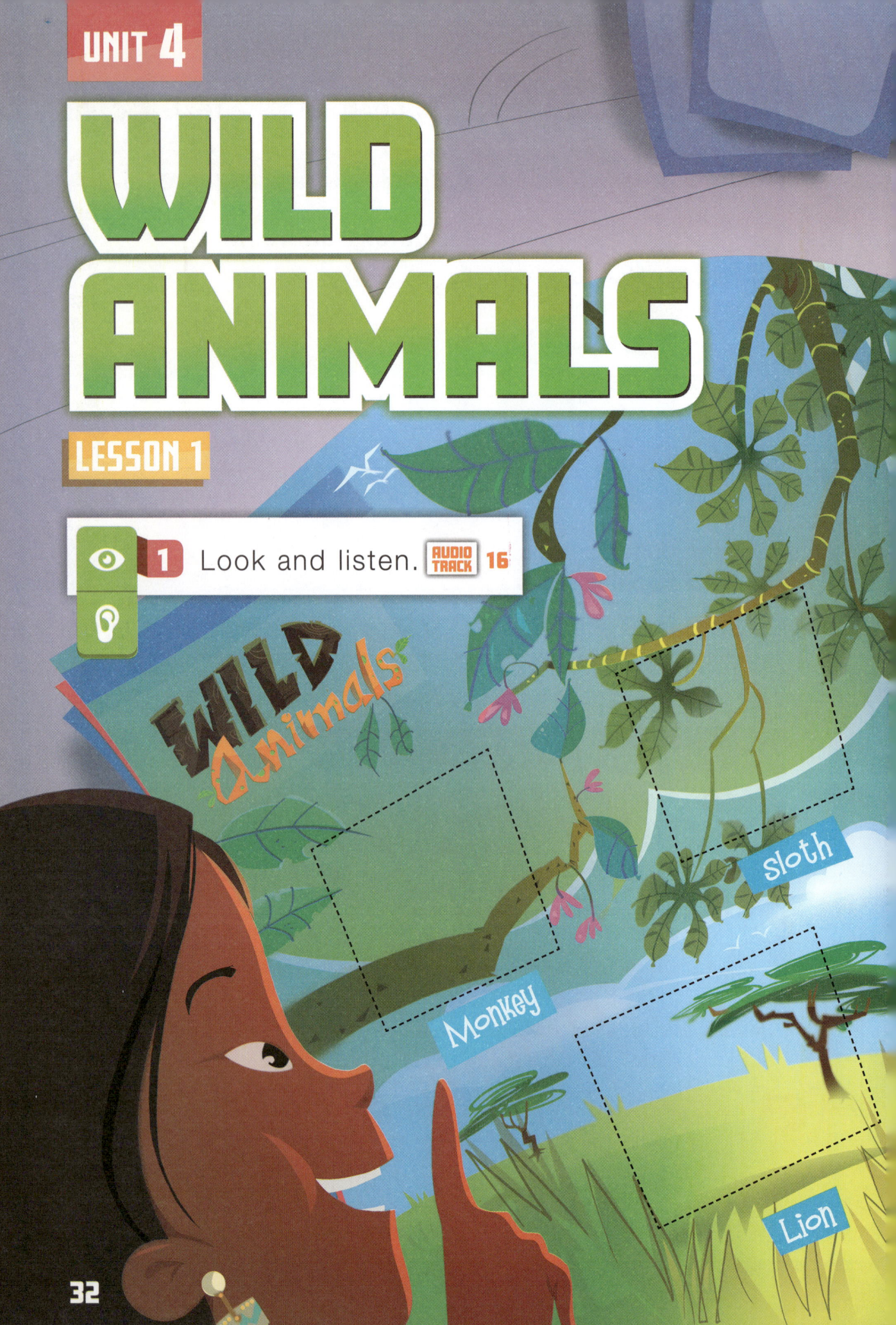

LESSON 2

1 Look and write.

a.

b.

c.

d.

e.

f.

g.

2 Listen and match. AUDIO TRACK 18 WORK BOOK 93

a. This animal is orange and brown. It has four legs and a long neck. It is tall and beautiful.

b. This animal is small and beautiful. It has a lot of hair. It is orange.

c. This animal is small. It has four legs and a tail.

d. This animal is very small. It has four short legs. It is white and brown.

LESSON 3

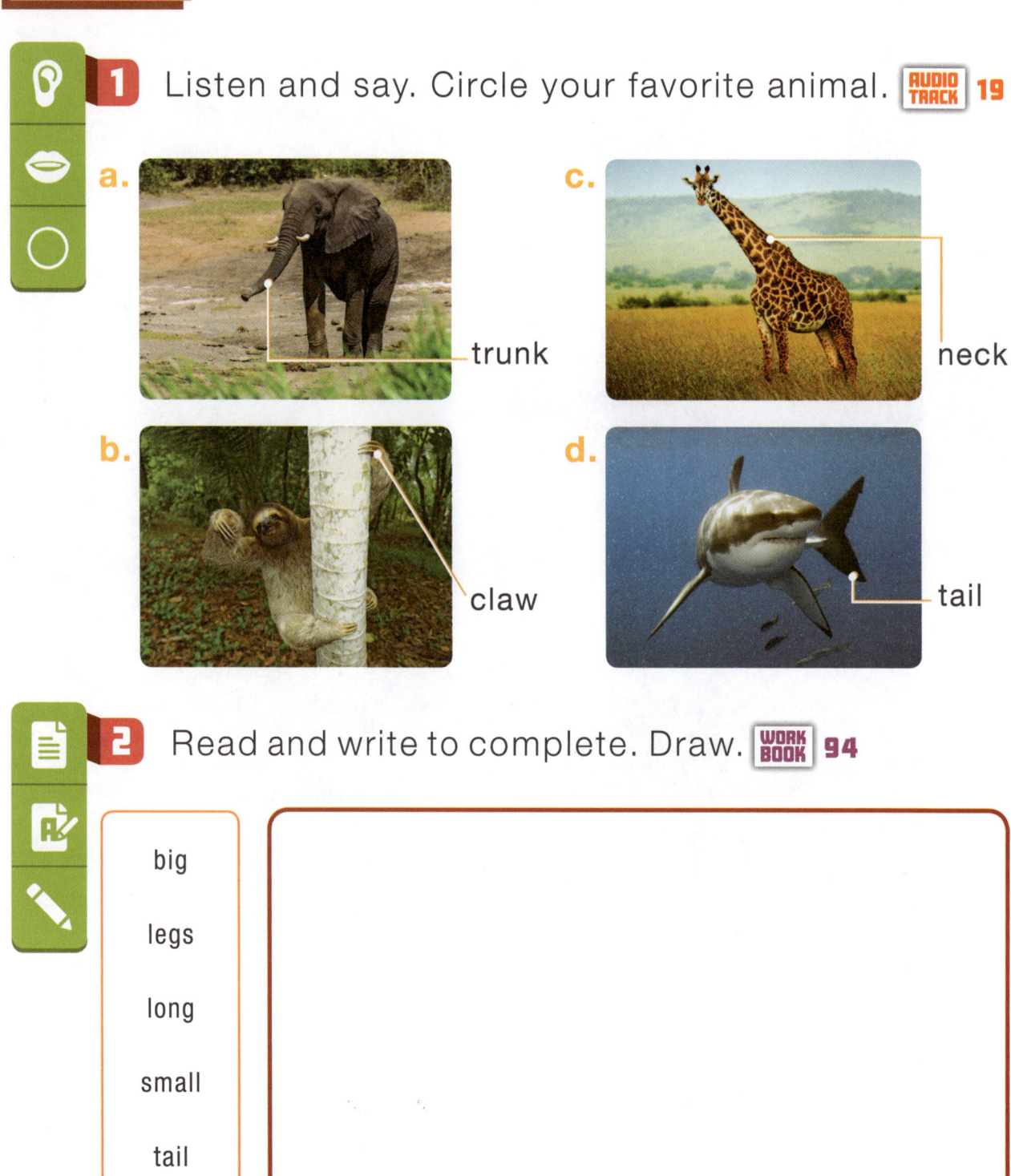

1 Listen and say. Circle your favorite animal. AUDIO TRACK 19

a. — trunk

b. — claw

c. — neck

d. — tail

2 Read and write to complete. Draw. WORKBOOK 94

big
legs
long
small
tail
trunk

a. The elephant has a long _____ and _____ ears.

b. The rabbit has _____ ears and a _____ mouth.

c. The lion has four _____ and a long _____.

OUR VALUES

Color.

LESSON 4

1 Read. Circle the words that complete the sentences.

a. The text has **stories** / **information** about an animal.

b. The animal in the text is a **wild animal** / **pet**.

Franciscana Fact Sheet
Pontoporia blainvillei
Type: mammal
Status: CR (critically endangered)
Size: small (1.6-1.7 m; 30 kg)
Color: brown or gray
Legs: no
Tail: yes
Claws: no
Diet: carnivore
Habitat: coastal Atlantic waters of Southeastern South America

Source: <www.fao.org/fishery/species/18234/en> and <www.icmbio.gov.br/portal/faunabrasileira/lista-de-especies/6138-especie-6138>. Accessed Feb. 20, 2019.

2 Read the fact sheet. Circle **YES** or **NO**.

a. The animal in the fact sheet is a shark.   YES   NO

b. The animal is brown or gray.   YES   NO

c. It has four legs.   YES   NO

d. It has a tail.   YES   NO

e. It eats only plants.   YES   NO

3 Read and write to complete. WORKBOOK 95

Blond Titi Monkey Fact Sheet

Callicebus barbarabrownae

Type: mammal

Status: CR (_____)

Size: _____ (80 cm; 1 kg)

Color: yellow, _____, orange, and _____

Number of legs: _____

Tail: _____

Claws: _____

Diet: omnivore

Habitat: Caatinga, Northeastern Brazil

Source: <www.icmbio.gov.br/portal/images/stories/docs-plano-de-acao/pan-primatas-caatinga/sumario-primatas-nordeste-web.pdf>. Accessed Feb. 20, 2019.

REVIEW 3·4

1 Listen. Check (✓) if the description matches the picture. AUDIO TRACK 20

a. 
b. 
c. 
d. 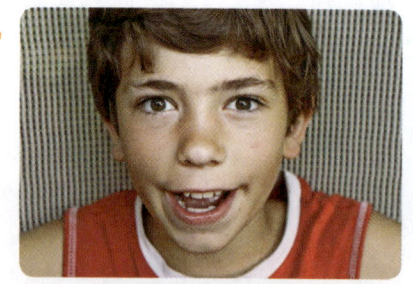
e. 
f.

2 Circle the word that completes each sentence.

a. My sister **has** / **have** long brown hair.
b. I **has** / **have** green eyes. I **has** / **have** short hair.
c. Arthur **has** / **have** blue eyes. He **has** / **have** blond hair.
d. Our teacher **has** / **have** short dark hair.

3 Look at the pictures. Complete the crossword puzzle.

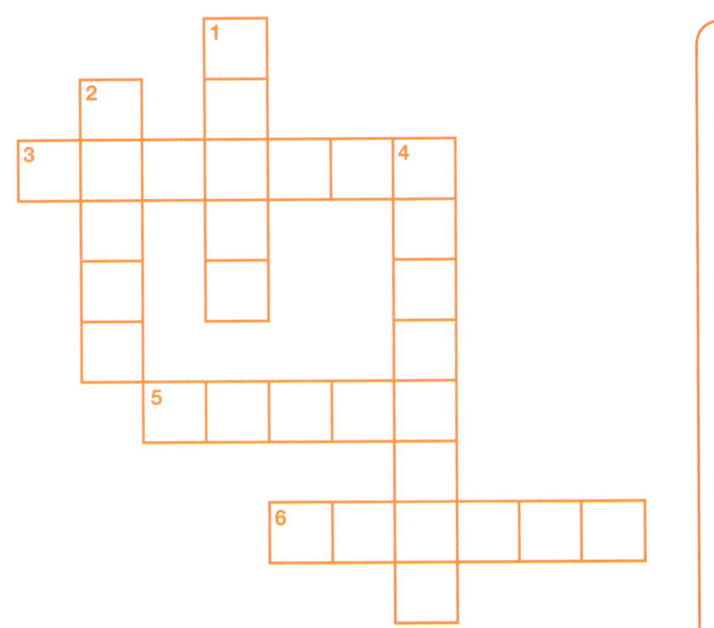

ACROSS →

3. (giraffe)
6. (monkey)
5. (sloth)

DOWN ↓

1. (shark)
2. (tiger)
4. (elephant)

4 Listen to your classmate and draw an animal.

"This animal is big. It has no legs. It has sharp teeth. It is gray."

UNIT 5

HOW MANY?

LESSON 1

1 Look and listen. 🎧 21

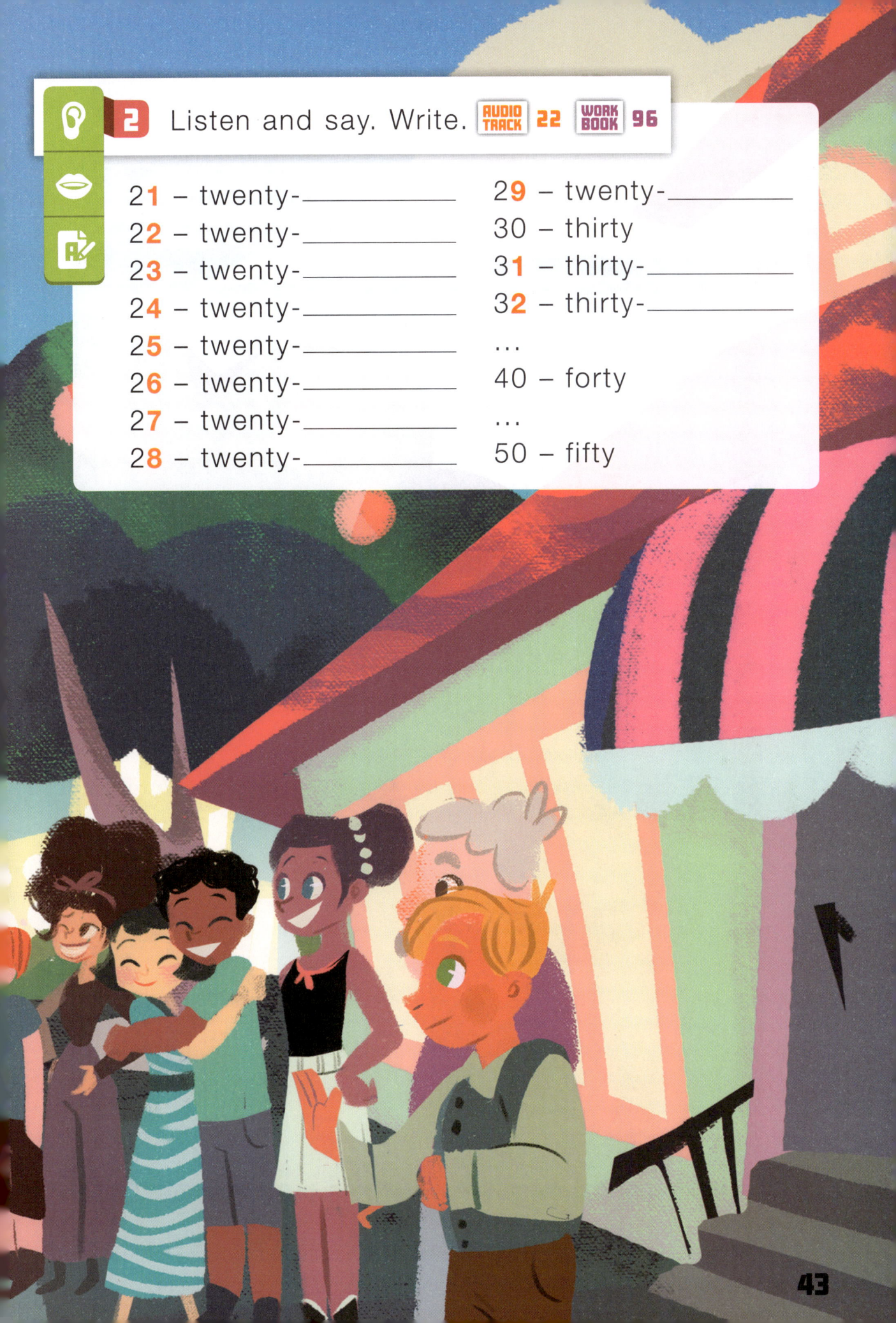

2 Listen and say. Write. AUDIO TRACK 22 WORKBOOK 96

2**1** – twenty-_____
2**2** – twenty-_____
2**3** – twenty-_____
2**4** – twenty-_____
2**5** – twenty-_____
2**6** – twenty-_____
2**7** – twenty-_____
2**8** – twenty-_____

2**9** – twenty-_____
30 – thirty
3**1** – thirty-_____
3**2** – thirty-_____
...
40 – forty
...
50 – fifty

LESSON 2

1 Listen and stick. AUDIO TRACK 23 STICK 118

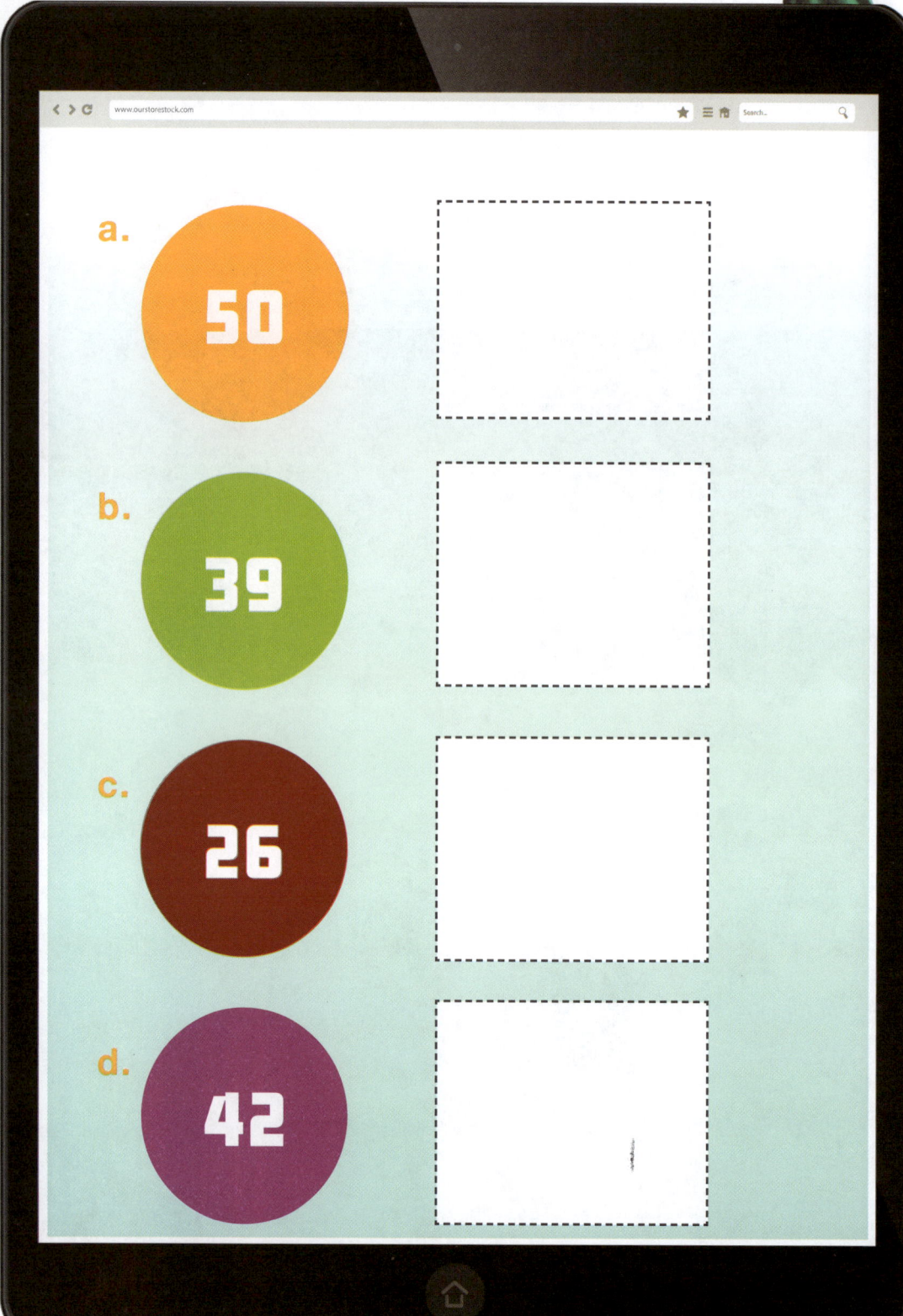

a. 50

b. 39

c. 26

d. 42

2 Listen and write. 🎧 24

a. 35 + 12 = _____

b. _____ = 40

c. _____ = 30

d. 50 − 17 = _____

e. 48 − 26 = _____

f. 21 + _____ = _____

g. 20 + _____ = 50

3 Look and write to complete. 📕 97

Even Numbers	Odd Numbers
0	1
2	
	5
	7
8	

Odds or evens?

Evens!

LESSON 3

1 Look and write.

Example: 24 – 28 – **thirty-two** – 36 – **forty**

a. 50 – _____ – 30 – 20 – _____
b. _____ – 20 – 25 – _____
c. 46 – 44 – _____ – 40 – _____
d. 11 – _____ – 15 – 17 – _____

2 Look and color.

a. 4 x 5 = _____ red
b. 6 x 5 = _____ green
c. 6 x 7 = _____ orange
d. 2 x 7 = _____ blue
e. 9 x 3 = _____ yellow
f. 10 x 5 = _____ black

3 Look and circle. WORKBOOK 98

"I have $27."

- Popcorn $12
- Cinema Ticket $15
- Drink $7
- Donut $5

a. 🎟 + 🍿 = _____ dollars.

b. 🎟 + 🥤 + 🍩 + 🍿 = _____.

c. 🎟 + 🍩 + 🥤 = _____.

OUR VALUES

Color.

LESSON 4

1 Read and find the information.

CineDark
Presenting
Ralph Breaks the Internet
3:15 p.m. Wen 3/13/19
K-31 $16.00
IMAX

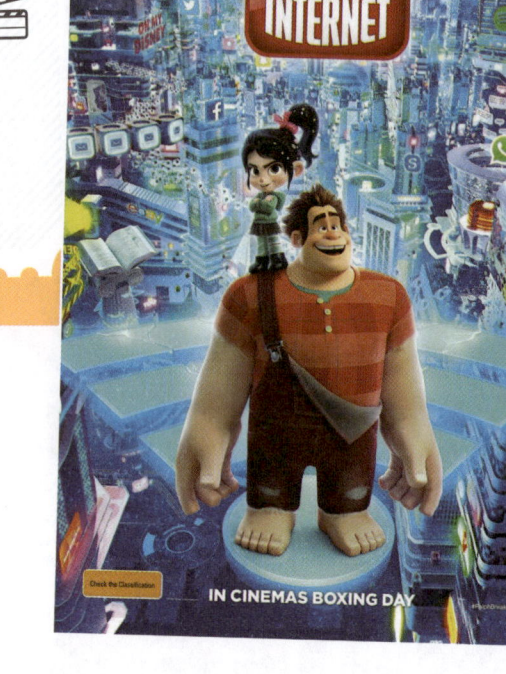

a. Movie: _____
b. Date: _____
c. Time: _____
d. Price: _____

2 Read the problem and write the solution.

Dad, mom, my brother, and I want to see Ralph Breaks the Internet. How much are the tickets for the family?

_____

3 Look. Read and write. WORKBOOK 99

- Time ◆ Price
- Seat ◆ Date
- Event

Ticket 1 (Basketball)

43	G	L13
Section	Box	

MIAMI WARRIORS vs. LOS ANGELES LIONS

Staples Arena | Los Angeles, CA

| April 26 | 8 p.m. | $37 |

Ticket 2 (Concert)

| Aug 5 | 7 p.m. | $80 |

ARIANA GRANDE

Staples Arena | Los Angeles, CA

Section **108** Box **E** **F4**

49

UNIT 6
MY ROUTINE

LESSON 1

1 Look and listen. AUDIO TRACK 25

My Routine

SUNDAY	MONDAY	TUESDAY	WEDNESDAY	THURSDAY	FRIDAY	SATURDAY
• Free!	• go to school, • walk the dog (Lisa), • do homework, • play soccer.	• go to school, • walk the dog (Jordan), • do homework, • ballet class.	• go to school, • walk the dog (Lisa and Jordan), • do homework, • watch TV.	• go to school, • walk the dog (Jordan), • do homework, • ballet class.	• go to school, • walk the dog (Lisa), • do homework, • play soccer.	• walk the dog (Jordan and Lisa), • play video game.

NOTES
HAVE A NICE DAY!

IMPORTANT
DO HOMEWORK!

2 Listen and say. AUDIO TRACK 26

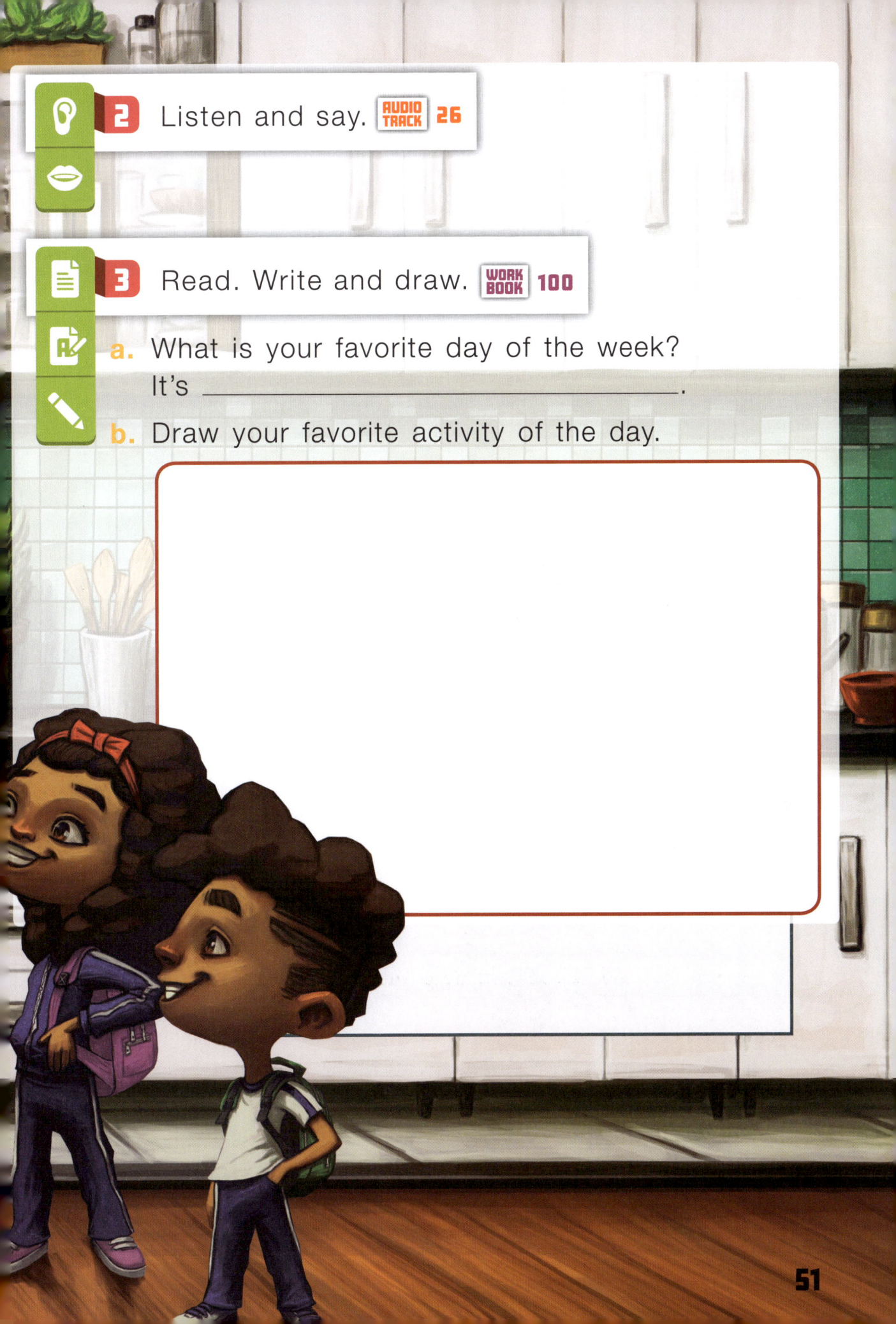

3 Read. Write and draw. WORKBOOK 100

a. What is your favorite day of the week?
   It's _____.

b. Draw your favorite activity of the day.

LESSON 2

1 Complete the table.

Yesterday	Today	Tomorrow
	Tuesday	
	Sunday	
	Thursday	
	Saturday	
	Monday	
	Friday	
	Wednesday	

2 Listen and match. AUDIO TRACK 27

a. Susan — Saturday

b. Tom — Tuesday

c. Amy — Friday

3 Read and stick. STICK 118 WORKBOOK 101

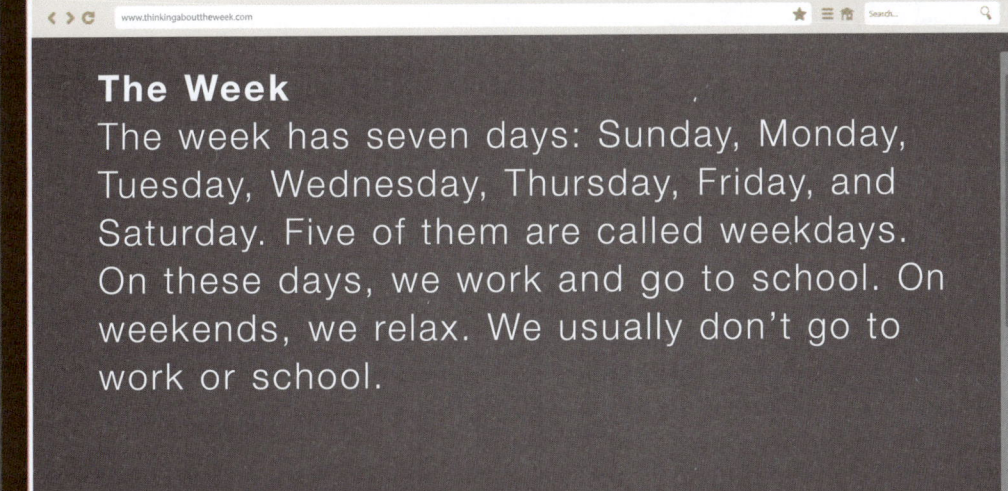

The Week
The week has seven days: Sunday, Monday, Tuesday, Wednesday, Thursday, Friday, and Saturday. Five of them are called weekdays. On these days, we work and go to school. On weekends, we relax. We usually don't go to work or school.

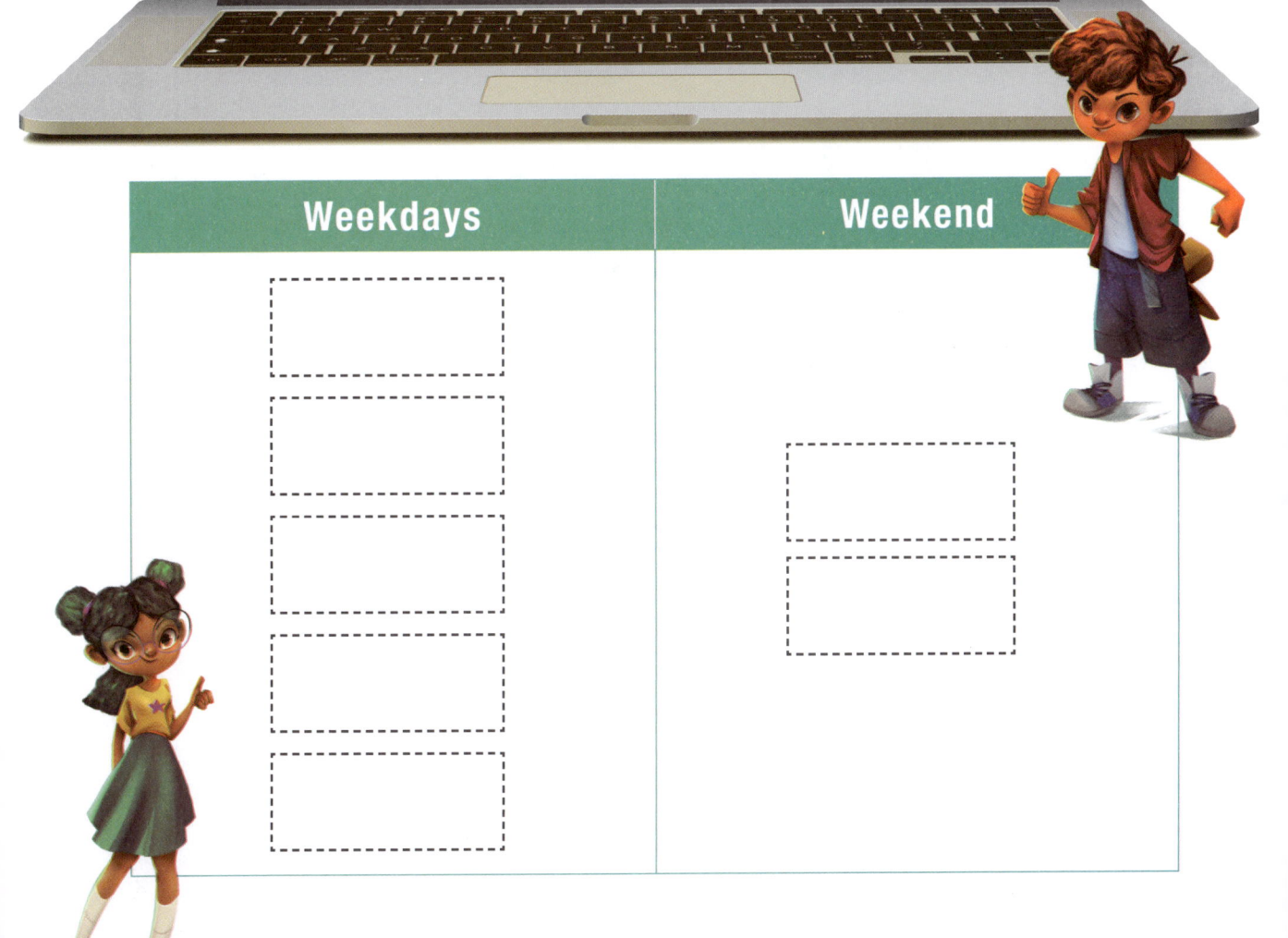

Weekdays	Weekend

LESSON 3

1 Read and listen. Write **T** (true) or **F** (false).

AUDIO TRACK 28   WORK BOOK 102

ORIGIN OF DAY NAMES

The Romans  named the days of the week with the Latin words for the Sun, the Moon, and five planets named in honor of Roman gods: Mars, Mercury, Jupiter, Venus, and Saturn.

In English we use the Latin names for Saturday, Sunday, and Monday. For the other days, the Nordic  gods have substituted the Roman gods: Tuesday honors Tiw, Wednesday honors Woden (or Odin), Thursday honors Thor, and Friday honors Frigg.

Source: <www.almanac.com/content/origin-day-names> and <www.webexhibits.org/calendars/week.html>. Accessed Feb. 25, 2019.

54

a. ☐ Five planets, the Sun, and the Moon are the names for the days of the week in Latin.

b. ☐ Sunday is the day of the Sun in Latin and English.

c. ☐ The names of the planets honor Nordic gods.

d. ☐ Monday honors the Moon.

e. ☐ The Nordic god Thor is honored on Tuesday.

OUR VALUES

Draw and color. **My Week**

Sun	Mon	Tue	Wed	Thu	Fri	Sat

LESSON 4

1 Read Dan's routine.

Hi, I'm Dan. I have a busy week. On Mondays, I have English tests. On Tuesdays and Thursdays, I go to soccer practice. On Fridays, I visit my grandma. On weekends, I play video games. And I go to school and do my homework on weekdays, of course.

2. Look and check (✓) Dan's weekly organizer.

a. ☐

SUN	MON	TUE	WED	THU	FRI	SAT
– Play video games	– Go to school – Play soccer – Do homework	– Go to school – English test	– Go to school – Play soccer – Do homework	– Go to school – Do homework	– Go to school – Do homework	– Play video games

b. ☐

SUN	MON	TUE	WED	THU	FRI	SAT
– Play video games	– Go to school – English test – Do homework	– Go to school – Play soccer – Do homework	– Go to school – Do homework	– Go to school – Play soccer – Do homework	– Go to school – Do homework – Visit grandma	– Play video games

3. Look and complete your weekly organizer. WORKBOOK 103

soccer

ballet class

make my bed

swimming class

walk the dog

watch TV

birthday party

play video games

REVIEW 5·6

1 Find and circle the days of the week. Then write.

```
A C M M N X O O D Y A K X
S D W Q K Y A D N O M A V
U C T M Z A Y H U C V Y D
N T U E W E D N E S D A Y
D A E H T O P L S V Y N I
A N S U Z W Q I D N O N R
Y A D S R U H T A W P O T
E S A T M R D O Y I K M G
Z X Y S A I O F R I D A Y
X S A A U R L L Y D K I E
Y S A T U R D A Y E O Y A
```

a. _____   e. _____

b. _____   f. _____

c. _____   g. _____

d. _____

2 Color the numbers and write the answers.

Number	Color
fourteen	blue and red
fifteen	orange and pink
thirteen	purple and green
twelve	green and yellow
fifty	gray and black
forty	orange and yellow
thirty	red and green
twenty	blue and white

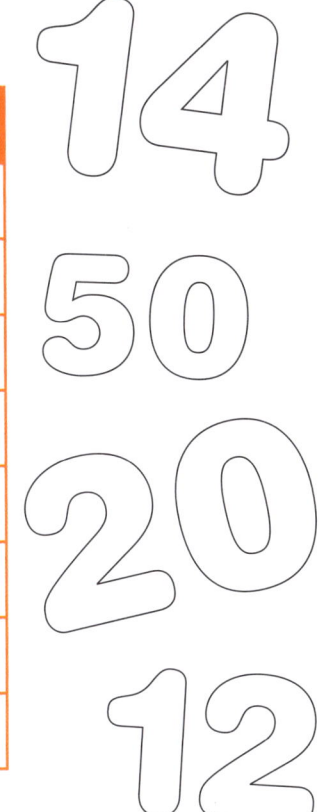

a. How many odd numbers are there in the table?

_____

b. How many even numbers are there in the table?

_____

3 Listen and write. AUDIO TRACK 29

a. _____ _____

b. _____ _____

c. _____ _____

d. _____ _____

e. _____ _____

UNIT 7
PLACES AROUND
LESSON 1

1 Look and listen. Point. AUDIO TRACK 30

2 Listen and say.

bakery — bank

mall — café

police station — park

restaurant — subway station

supermarket — store

3 Find and write.

61

LESSON 2

1 Listen and number. AUDIO TRACK 32

a. ☐   b. ☐   c.  ☐   d. ☐

2 Look and match.

bakery ♦ bank ♦ park ♦ store

a. _____

b. _____

c. _____

d. _____

62

3 Look and answer: Where is Anna? WORKBOOK 105

a. She's at a _____.

b. She's at a _____.

c. She's at a _____.

d. She's at a _____.

e. She's at a _____.

LESSON 3

1 Look and read.

The store is **next to** the supermarket.

The bank is **between** the restaurant and the café.

The bakery is **across from** the park.

The dog is **in front of** the mall.

2 Look at the map and complete.

across from
between
in front of
next to

a. The store is _____ the restaurant and the bank.
b. The bus stop is _____ the café.
c. The mall is _____ the park.
d. The police station is _____ the supermarket.

64

3 Listen and stick. AUDIO TRACK 33 STICK 119 WORKBOOK 106

OUR VALUES

Play.

65

LESSON 4

1 Look at the map. Write.

= lake, river, or sea
= park
// = street

- S-Mart
- Ann's
- Gray Station
- Smart Clothes
- Sweet Bread
- First National Bank
- The Plaza Mall
- The Good Food

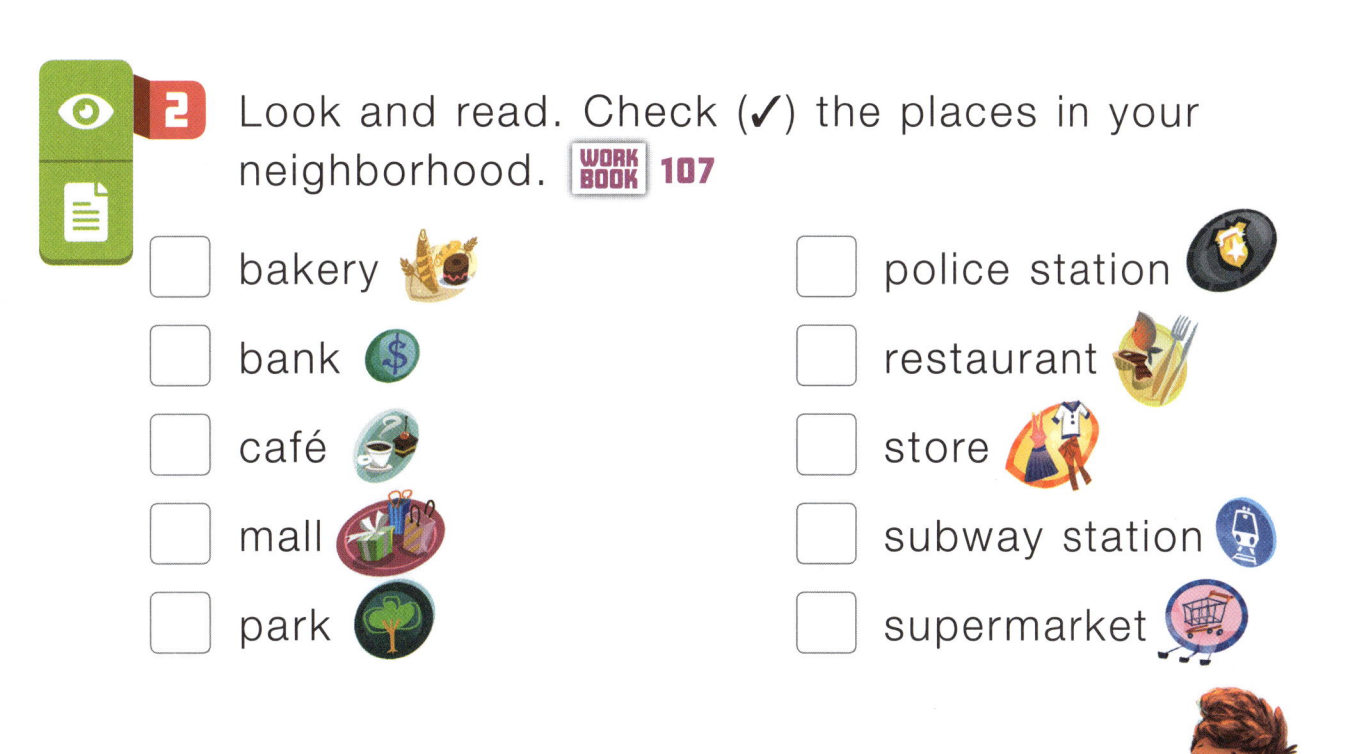

2 Look and read. Check (✓) the places in your neighborhood. WORKBOOK 107

- [ ] bakery
- [ ] bank
- [ ] café
- [ ] mall
- [ ] park
- [ ] police station
- [ ] restaurant
- [ ] store
- [ ] subway station
- [ ] supermarket

3 Look and draw. Make a map of your neighborhood.

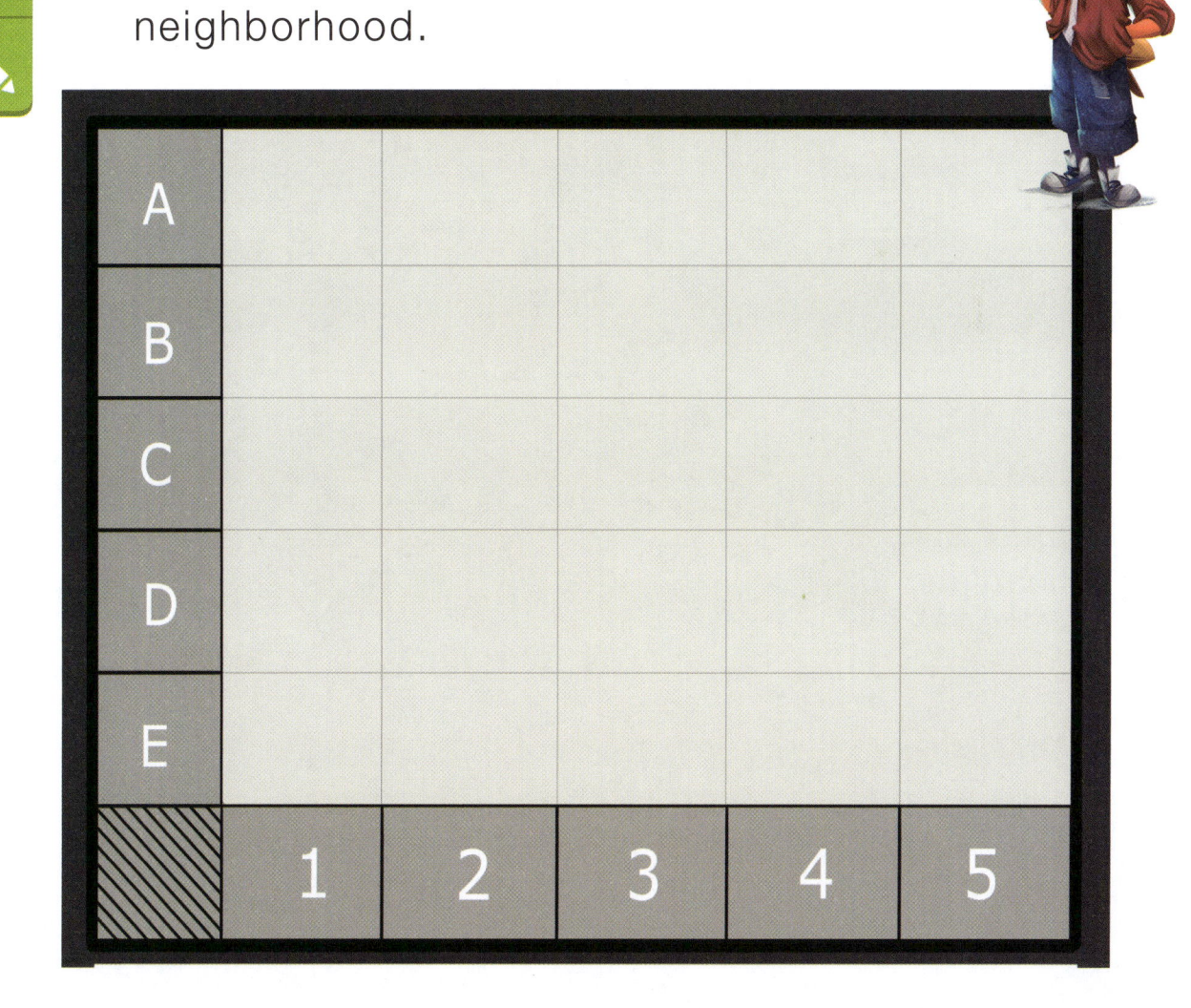

	1	2	3	4	5
A					
B					
C					
D					
E					

UNIT 8
YUMMY!

LESSON 1

👁️ 👂 **1** Look and listen. AUDIO TRACK 34

water

chocolate

cookies

2 Listen and find. Point and say. AUDIO TRACK 35

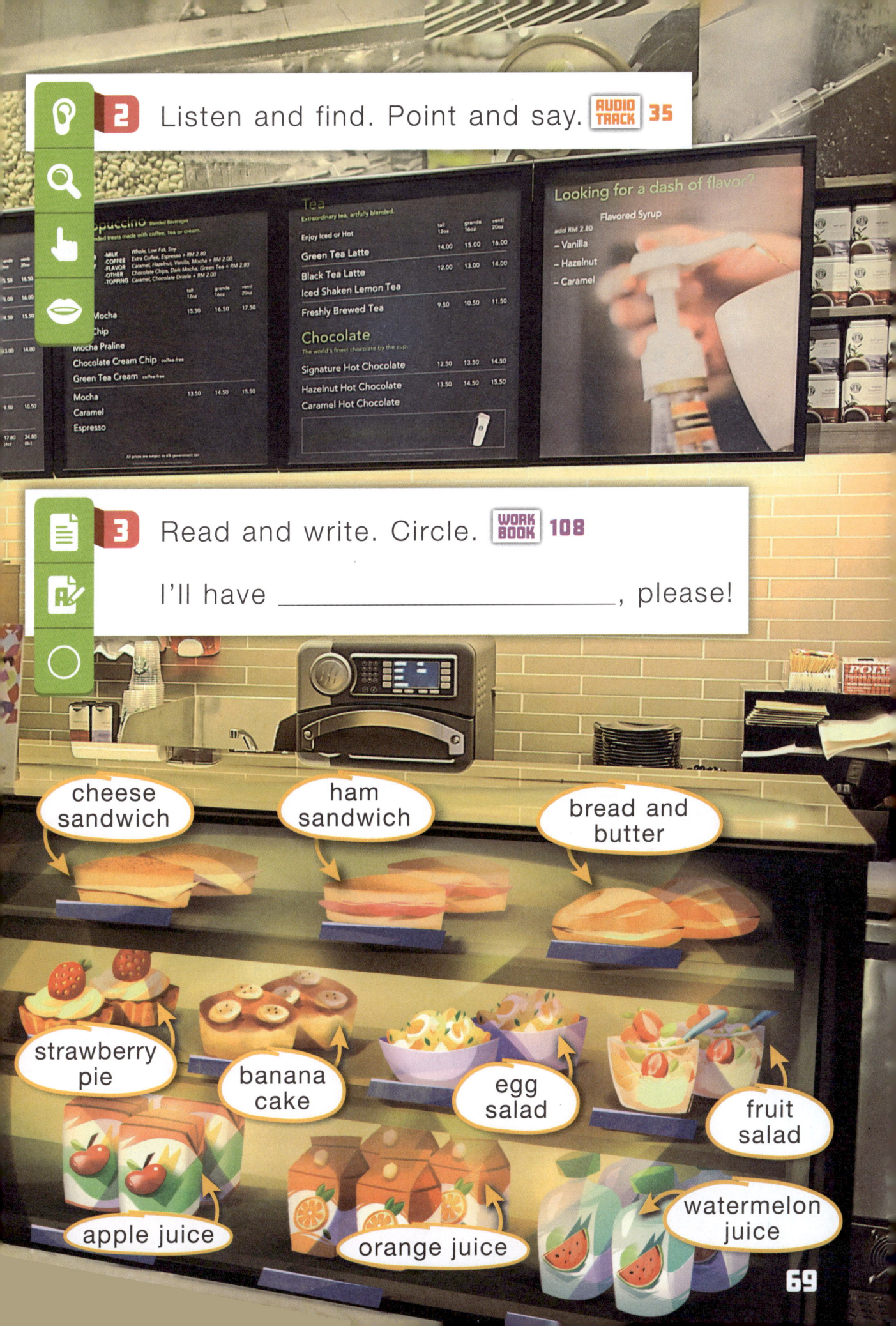

3 Read and write. Circle. WORK BOOK 108

I'll have _____, please!

- cheese sandwich
- ham sandwich
- bread and butter
- strawberry pie
- banana cake
- egg salad
- fruit salad
- apple juice
- orange juice
- watermelon juice

LESSON 2

1 Look and read. Write.

chocolate — strawberry — orange — egg — ham — cheese

a. juice: _____

b. pie: _____

c. cookie: _____

d. cake: _____

e. sandwich: _____

2 Read and draw.

POP CAFÉ

2 cheese sandwiches $8.80
1 apple pie $4.50
1 orange juice $3.60
1 fruit salad $2.25

Receipt
Total $19.15
===============

70

3 Read and write. WORKBOOK 109

> bread ♦ cheese ♦ chocolate ♦ coffee
> egg ♦ ham ♦ pie ♦ strawberry

Food

a. _____ and _____ sandwich

b. _____ and butter

c. apple _____

d. _____ salad sandwich

Drinks

e. _____ juice

f. _____ with milk

g. hot _____

LESSON 3

1 Look and read.

> An apple pie and a coffee, please!

> Sure!

2 Complete with **a** or **an**. Listen and check. Say.
AUDIO TRACK 36

___ orange juice, please.

___ strawberry pie, please.

___ apple juice, please.

___ cheese sandwich, please.

___ hot chocolate, please.

___ egg sandwich, please.

3. Write the food in the appropriate basket.

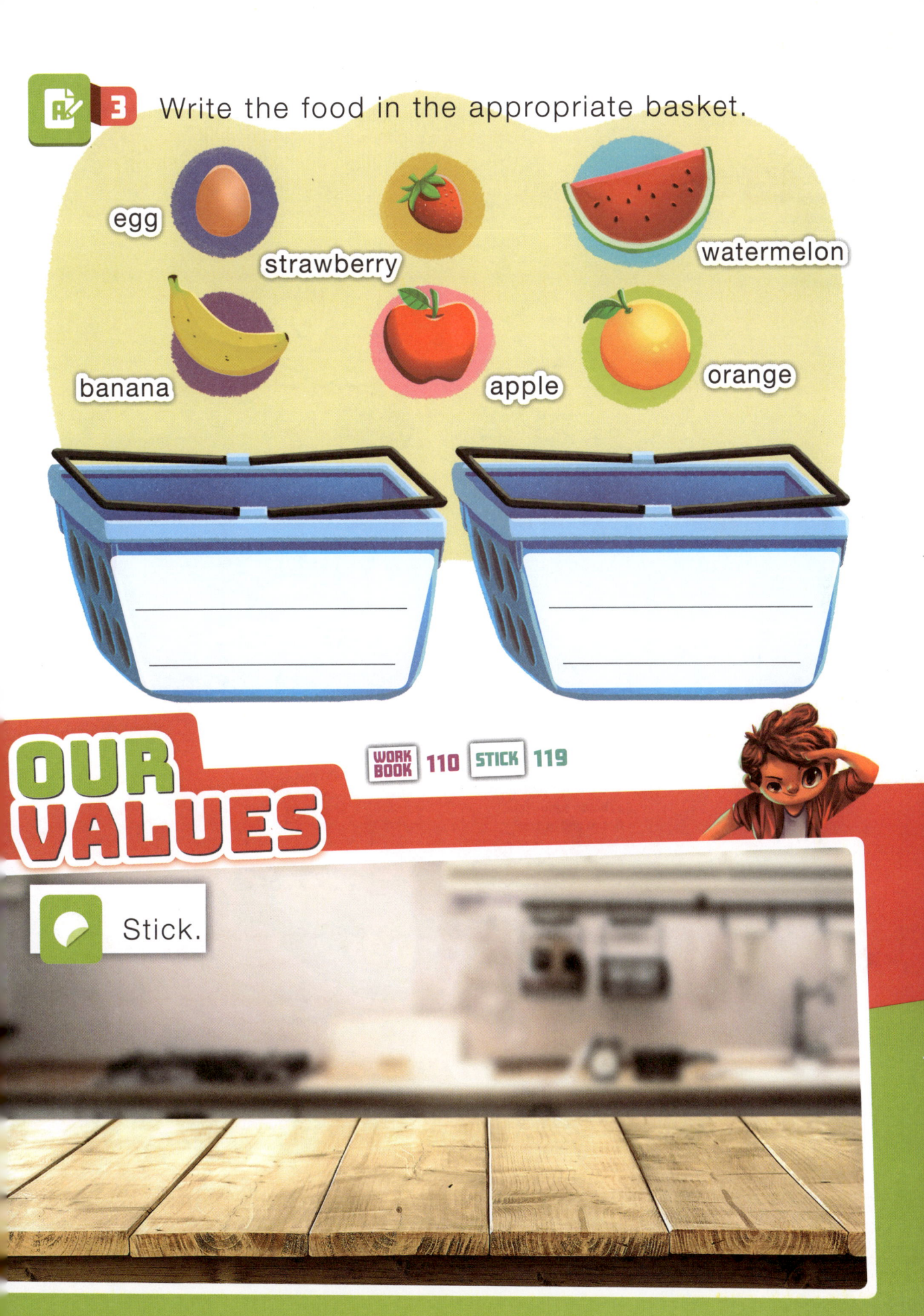

- egg
- strawberry
- watermelon
- banana
- apple
- orange

WORK BOOK 110   STICK 119

OUR VALUES

Stick.

LESSON 4

1 Look and read.

POP CAFÉ MENU
DELICIOUS AND HEALTHY MEALS FOR KIDS

ENJOY!!

Salads
Green salad
Ceasar salad

$3.99

Snacks
Ham and cheese sandwich
Egg salad sandwich
Bread and butter

$4.99

Desserts
Orange Cake
Chocolate Pie
Strawberry Pie

$1.99

Fruits
Apple
Watermelon

$2.99

Drinks
Juice (Orange or Tangerine)
Coffee
Milk
Hot Chocolate
Water

$1.99

2 Read the menu and write the answers. WORKBOOK 111

a.	Name of the café	
b.	Sections on the menu	
c.	Types of sandwiches	
d.	Price of the desserts	
e.	Types of pies	
f.	Types of juice	

3 Look and write.

Kids menu

Main Dishes
_____
_____
_____
_____

Special menu
_____
_____

Drinks
_____
_____
_____
_____

Desserts
_____
_____

DELICIOUS HEALTHY MEALS FOR KIDS

Yummy!

WELCOME TO OUR TASTY FOOD MENU

9.00 AM. - 9.00 PM.
OPEN EVERYDAY
TEL. 2000 25 1234

REVIEW 7·8

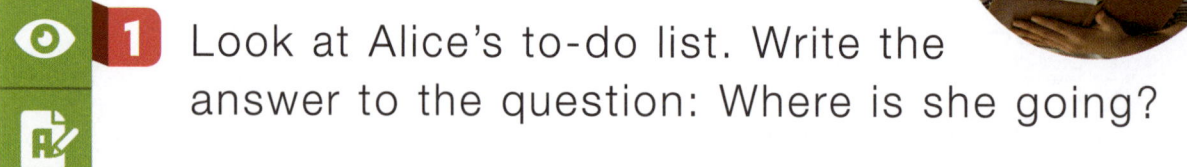

1 Look at Alice's to-do list. Write the answer to the question: Where is she going?

Alice's to-do list:
- Have ☕ with Amanda.
- Get 💵
- Buy a new 👕
- Buy 🥖
- Take Buddy to the 🛝
- Have 🍕 with Mom at Gennaro's.

bakery ◆ bank ◆ café
park ◆ restaurant ◆ store

a. _____
b. _____
c. _____
d. _____
e. _____
f. _____

2 Listen and match the places with their names.
AUDIO TRACK 37

☐ bank   ☐ bus stop   ☐ mall   ☐ store

76

3 Circle food and drink items in the word spiral.

STRAWBERRY COFFEE CHOCOLATE EGG HAM BREAD CHEESE

4 Write the words from **Activity 3** in the chart.

Food	Drinks

5 Write the food and drinks you like or don't like.

☺	☹

GLOSSARY

UNIT 1 A, B, C ...

A B C D E F G H I J K L M
N O P Q R S T U V W X Y Z

UNIT 2 FAMILY PICTURE

- grandpa
- grandma 
- mom 
- dad 
- son 
- niece 
- nephew 
- daughter 
- cousins 
- aunt 
- uncle 

UNIT 3 LOOKS

- blond hair — brown eyes
- black hair — blue eyes
- gray hair — green eyes
- brown hair — dark eyes
- red hair — green eyes

UNIT 4 WILD ANIMALS

- elephant
- lion 
- shark 
- tiger 
- sloth 
- giraffe 
- monkey

UNIT 5 HOW MANY?

21 – twenty-one 26 – twenty-six 31 – thirty-one
22 – twenty-two 27 – twenty-seven 32 – thirty-two
23 – twenty-three 28 – twenty-eight ...
24 – twenty-four 29 – twenty-nine 40 – forty
25 – twenty-five 30 – thirty ...
         50 – fifty

UNIT 6 MY ROUTINE

MONDAY	TUESDAY	WEDNESDAY	THURSDAY	FRIDAY	SATURDAY	SUNDAY

UNIT 7 PLACES AROUND

bakery  bank  café  mall  park

police station  restaurant  store  subway station  supermarket

UNIT 8 YUMMY!

cheese sandwich  egg salad  ham sandwich  water chocolate cookies

bread and butter  banana cake  strawberry pie  fruit salad

WORKBOOK

UNIT 1 **LESSON 1**

Complete the crossword puzzle.

ACROSS →

2.  (soccer ball) 3.  (doll) 5.  (spinning top) 6.  (board game) 8.  (car)

DOWN ↓

1.  (play dough)
2.  (blocks)
4.  (boy)
7.  (girl)

Across:
2. B _ LL
3. D _ LL
5. S P _ N N _ N G T _ P
6. G _ M _
8. C _ R

Down:
1. P L _ Y D _ _ H
2. B _ _ L D _ N G   B L _ C K S
4. B _ Y
7. G _ R L

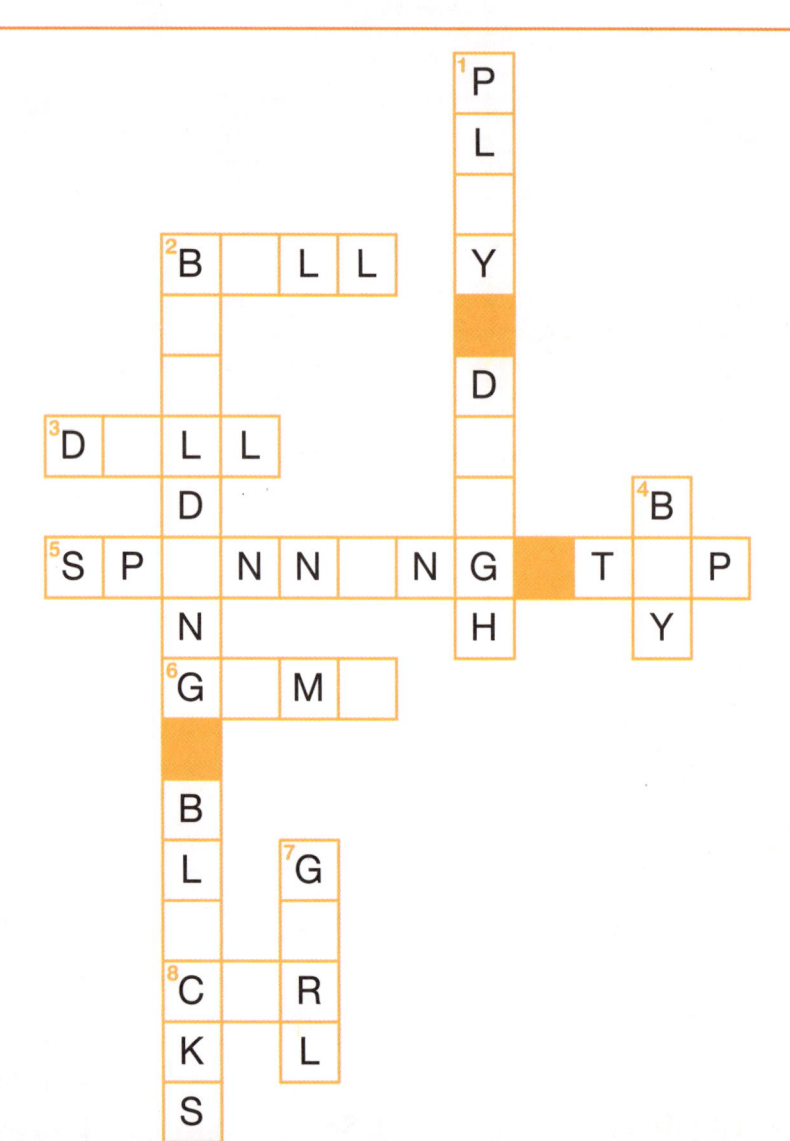

LESSON 2

1. Look at the pictures and write the answers.

a. What's this?

It's a _____.

b. What's this?

It's a _____.

c. What's this?

It's a _____.

d. What's this?

It's a _____.

e. What's this?

It's a _____.

f. What's this?

It's a _____.

2. Write the words from **Activity 1** in alphabetical order.

_____   _____

_____   _____

_____   _____

LESSON 3

Read and complete the sentences.

a. This is my new _____.

b. This is Buddy, my _____.

c. A, E, I, O, and U are _____.

d. How do you say "caneta" in _____?

e. _____ is my favorite color.

f. Tom is a _____.

g. B, C, D, F are _____.

LESSON 4

1. Look at the pictures. Complete the words.

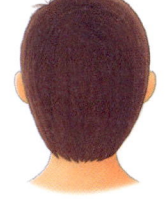

a. sh__p ✗ sh__ __p

b. __at ✗ __at

c. __ed ✗ __ead

2. Write and draw a comic strip.

83

WORKBOOK

UNIT 2 **LESSON 1**

> This is my family.

👁 Look and unscramble the words.

a. This is my NAUT.

b. This is my CELUN.

_____   _____

c. These are my UOSSICN.

d. This is my mom's ENEIC.

e. This is my mom's PEHEWN.

_____   _____   _____

84

LESSON 2

Look at the family tree and complete the paragraph.

Hi, my name's Zach and this is my family. James and Harriet are my (a) _____ and (b) _____. Andrew and Louise are my (c) _____ and (d) _____. Julia is my (e) _____. Anna and Emily are my (f) _____ and John is my (g) _____. Josh is my (h) _____.

LESSON 3

Read the clues and write the names in the family tree.

Ryan   Monica

a. Brian is Thomas's nephew. Katherine is also his aunt.
b. Janice has a son and two daughters. Elizabeth is one of her daughters.
c. Monica is Patrick and Ryan's cousin.
d. Thomas is Gerard's son and Elizabeth's brother.
e. Katherine has three nephews and two nieces.
f. Mary and Thomas have two sons.
g. Michelle's father is Anthony.
h. Gerard is Katherine's dad.
i. Anthony is Ryan and Patrick's uncle.

LESSON 4

Look, read, and match.

a.

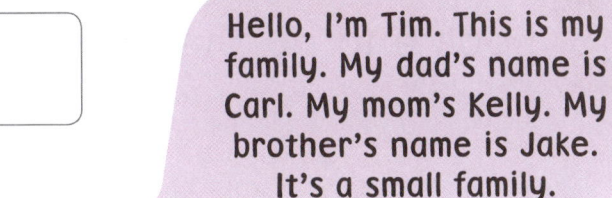

Hello, I'm Tim. This is my family. My dad's name is Carl. My mom's Kelly. My brother's name is Jake. It's a small family.

b.

Hi, I'm Mia. This is my family. Elisa is my mom and David is my dad. I have one brother, Lucas, and a little sister, Makayla.

c.

Hello! I'm Arjun. This is a picture of my family. Look! My grandpa and my grandma. My mom and dad. My uncle and aunt. My little sister is on my grandpa's lap. I'm with my dad. We're a big family.

d.

Hi, my name's Jen. This is an old family picture. My mom is this little girl on the right. This is her brother, my uncle Mike. And these are my grandpa and grandma, Gerry and Hannah.

WORKBOOK

UNIT 3 **LESSON 1**

👁 Look and do the crossword puzzle.

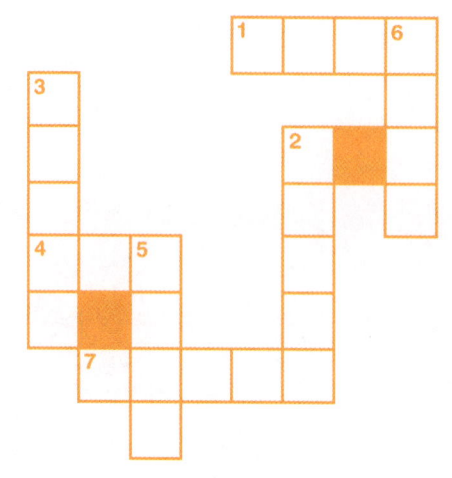

Across →

1. _____ hair 
4. _____ hair 
7. _____ eyes

Down ↓

2. _____ hair 
3. _____ hair 
5. _____ eyes 
6. _____ hair

LESSON 2

Write the sentences in the speech bubbles.

| He has short gray hair and dark eyes. | She has short black hair and dark eyes. |

| I have dark eyes and short black hair. | I have long black hair and brown eyes. |

My name's Miguel.
_____
_____
_____

This is Alice.
_____
_____
_____

Hello. My name is Susie.
_____
_____
_____

This is Mr. Pereira.
_____
_____
_____

LESSON 3

1. Read and complete the sentences with *have* or *has*.

a. My dad _____ short hair, but my mom _____ long hair.

b. My grandpa _____ gray hair, but my grandma _____ blond hair.

c. I _____ green eyes and brown hair.

d. My brother _____ dark hair.

e. Lily _____ long hair.

f. My PE teacher _____ brown eyes. Just like me! I _____ brown eyes too!

2. Read. Draw and color.

> My name is Jessica. I'm eight years old. I have long brown hair and green eyes.

LESSON 4

1. Look and create a character for a book.

My Character	
Name	
Age	
Hair Color	
Eye Color	

_____

_____

2. Draw a picture of yourself and write about you.

Me	
Name	
Age	
Hair Color	
Eye Color	

_____

_____

WORKBOOK

UNIT 4 **LESSON 1**

✏️ Write the names of the animals.

a.

b.

c.

d.

e.

f.

g.

LESSON 2

1. Complete with *is* or *has*. Match.

a. This animal _____ big. It _____ four legs. It _____ beautiful. It _____ orange and black.

b. This animal _____ small. It _____ four legs.

c. This animal _____ orange. It _____ a lot of hair. It _____ small and very beautiful.

d. This animal _____ no legs. It _____ gray and big.

e. This animal _____ tall. It _____ beautiful. It _____ four legs. It _____ orange and brown.

2. Write about an animal.

This animal is _____ It's _____.
It has _____.

LESSON 3

1. Look and unscramble the words.

a. tehet

c. sleg

e. cken

b. ntrku

d. sera

f. scwal

2. Circle the words that complete the sentences.

a. An elephant has big **ears** / **claws** and a long **trunk** / **neck**.

b. A shark has sharp **claws** / **teeth**.

c. A rabbit has long **ears** / **legs** and big **eyes** / **claws**.

d. A giraffe has a long **neck** / **head** and long **legs** / **teeth**.

LESSON 4

Read and circle **YES** or **NO**.

GOLDEN LION TAMARIN FACT SHEET

Leontopithecus rosalia

Type: mammal

Status: EN (endangered)

Size: small (26 cm; 600 g)

Color: orange

Number of legs: 4

Tail: yes

Claws: no

Diet: omnivore

Habitat: tropical rainforest in southeastern Brazil

Based on <http://www.nationalgeographic.com/animals/mammals/g/golden-lion-tamarin/>. Accessed Mar. 1st, 2019.

a. The animal in the fact sheet is a type of monkey.   YES / NO

b. The animal is brown.   YES / NO

c. It has two ears.   YES / NO

d. It has a tail.   YES / NO

e. It eats plants.   YES / NO

f. It is from Brazil.   YES / NO

WORKBOOK
UNIT 5 — LESSON 1

Look and do the crossword puzzle.

Across →
2. ~~29~~
4. 27
5. 38
8. 25
9. 21

Down ↓
1. 30
3. 23
4. 34
6. 36
7. 42

LESSON 2

1. Calculate. Find the results in the word search.

a. 20 + 4 = ☐

b. 7 × 4 = ☐

c. 50 − 18 = ☐

d. 9 × 4 = ☐

e. 25 + 16 = ☐

f. 33 + 10 = ☐

g. 9 × 5 = ☐

h. 50 − 3 = ☐

i. 22 + 27 = ☐

j. 25 + 25 = ☐

```
Z F T O Y R H H K E H N E R
H O H Q T W F X P B U H K F
S R I S D C T I P P E Y V O
K T R F S P W F F E N Y Y R
Y Y T N O D E I R T H Y R T
Z F Y B O R N H D O Y G P Y
B I T W E N T Y F O U R F N
I V W I Y Y Y Y P P L I O I
C E O F T H E J S X H A R N
Q A V R Y S I H F E M V T E
G F O D I Q G T Q W V G Y Z
J F D K N U H B K X P E O P
F D T H I R T Y S I X T N L
O A G U X R H F C O O Y E L
```

2. Write the answers from Activity 1 in the table.

Evens	Odds
a.	f.
b.	g.
c.	h.
d.	i.
e.	j.

LESSON 3

Look and solve the problems. Write the answers.

a. Five kids have five marbles each. What's the total number of marbles?

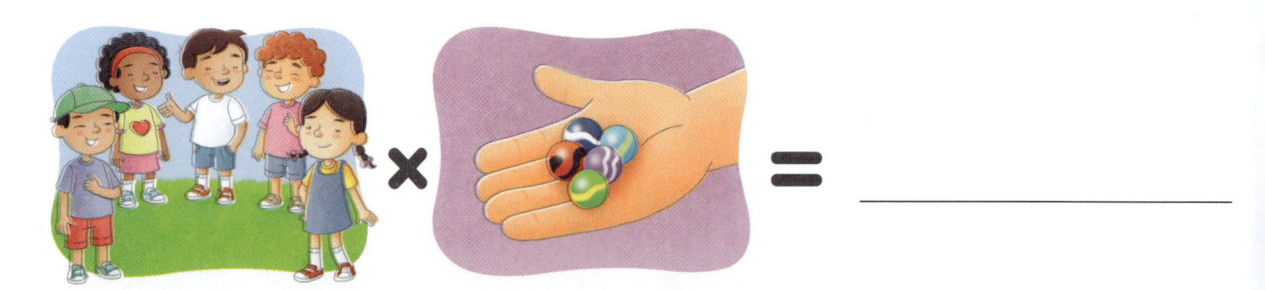

× = _____

b. Tanya's mom orders seven pizzas for Tanya's birthday party. Each pizza has five slices. How many slices of pizza are there?

× = _____

c. I see eight elephants at the lake. How many legs do I see?

× = _____

LESSON 4

Read the ticket. Match the words with the information.

a. Movie Mark ☐ day of the week

b. Star Games ☐ room number

c. 2:30 p.m. ☐ date

d. Saturday ☐ movie theater

e. 12-6-2019 ☐ seat

f. $7.50 ☐ title

g. J13 ☐ price

h. Theater 9 ☐ time

WORKBOOK

UNIT 6 LESSON 1

1. Look and find out the day of the week in each speech bubble.

→	▬	◆	▲	✪	★	☽	●	♦	✖	⬈	⤴	▪	▫	✧
A	D	E	F	H	I	M	N	O	R	S	T	U	W	Y

a. My favorite day of the week is ⤴▪◆⬈▬→✧.

_____

b. My favorite day of the week is ▫◆▬●◆⬈▬→✧.

_____

c. My favorite day of the week is ▲✖★▬→✧.

_____

d. My favorite day of the week is ⤴✪▪✖⬈▬→✧.

_____

e. My favorite day of the week is ☽♦●▬→✧.

_____

f. My favorite day of the week is ▲✖★▬→✧.

_____

g. My favorite day of the week is ⬈▪●▬→✧.

_____

2. Write the days of the week from Activity 1 in order.

1. Sunday	5. _____
2. _____	6. _____
3. _____	7. _____
4. _____	

LESSON 2

1. Match the calendar pages with the days of the week.

Tuesday

Thursday

Saturday

Monday

Sunday

Wednesday

Friday

2. Look at the pictures and write the answers.

a. You: What's your favorite day of the week, Jake?

   Jake: It's _____.
   I play volleyball.

b. You: What's your favorite day of the week, Sofia?

   Sofia: It's _____.
   I go swimming.

c. You: What's your favorite day of the week, Julia?

   Julia: It's _____.
   I visit my grandma.

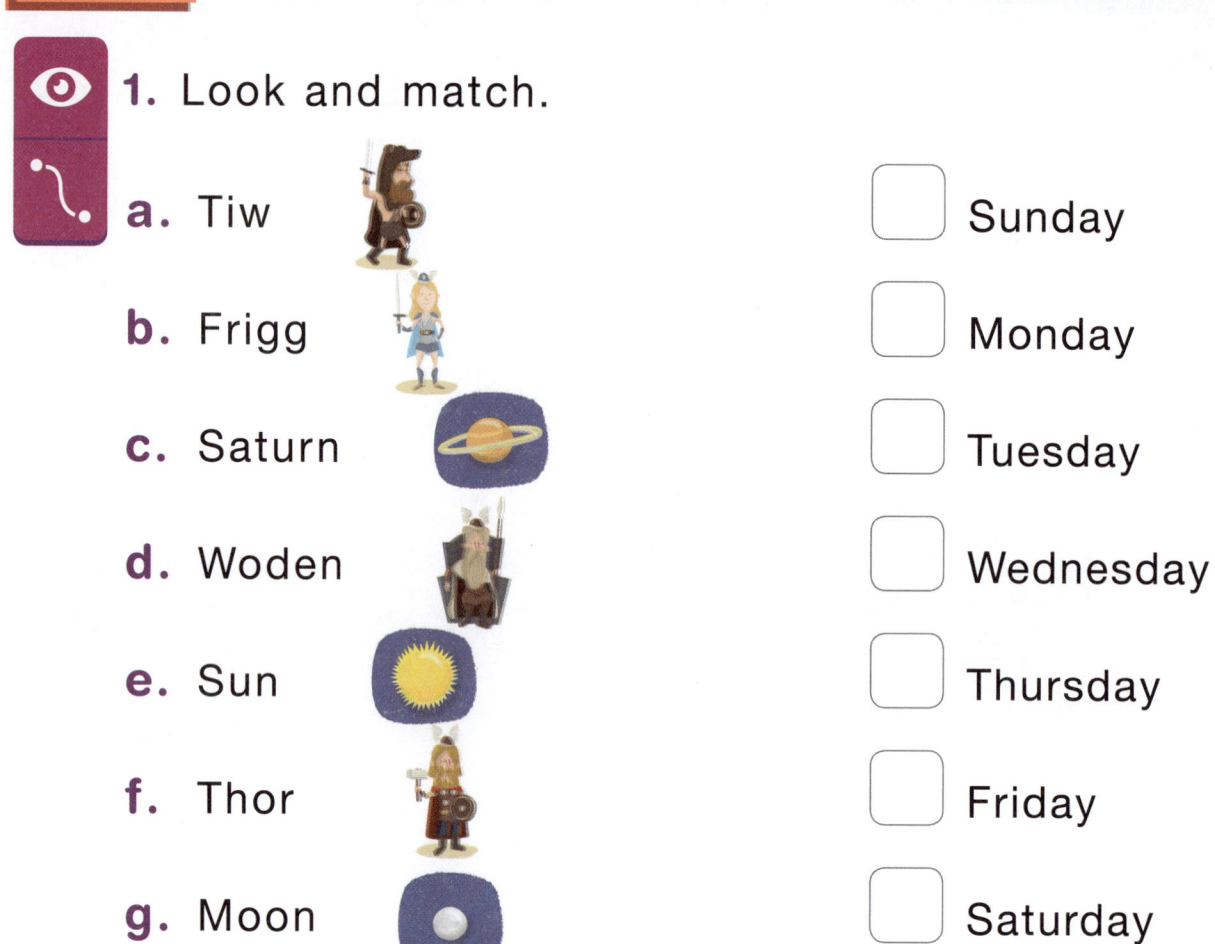

LESSON 3

1. Look and match.

a. Tiw
b. Frigg
c. Saturn
d. Woden
e. Sun
f. Thor
g. Moon

☐ Sunday
☐ Monday
☐ Tuesday
☐ Wednesday
☐ Thursday
☐ Friday
☐ Saturday

2. Write the names of the planets.

a. _____ b. _____ c. _____ d. _____

e. _____ f. _____ g. _____ h. _____

LESSON 4

1. Rewrite the sentences. Follow the example.

What do you do on Saturdays?	What do you do on Sundays?
a. Jess: I have	**e.** John: I play
I have ballet class.	_____
b. Bill: I	**f.** Mia: I
_____	_____
c. Maria: I	**g.** Mike: I
_____	_____
d. Dan: I	**h.** Bea: I
_____	_____

2. Read about Ann's week. Complete her organizer.

Hi, my name's Ann. I have a very busy week. On Mondays and Wednesdays, I play soccer. On Tuesdays and Thursdays, I have swimming classes. On Fridays, I have ballet classes. On Saturdays, I play video games, and on Sundays, I walk my dog, Fluffy!

Ann's Week

Monday	Tuesday	Wednesday	Thursday	Friday	Saturday	Sunday
Soccer	_____	_____	Swimming class	_____	_____	_____

103

WORKBOOK

UNIT 7 **LESSON 1**

Look some pictures and write the name of the places.

Mall • Café • Store • Bakery • Supermarket • Subway Station

a. _____

b. _____

c. _____

d. _____

e. _____

f. _____

LESSON 2

👁 Look at the pictures and guess the places.

a. Where's Jack?

_____

b. Where's Vivi?

_____

c. Where's Charlie?

_____

d. Where's Luke?

_____

e. Where's Gabe?

_____

LESSON 3

Look. Unscramble the words and rewrite the sentences.

a. The ABRKEY is next to the ANTRETURSA.

_____

b. The FACÉ is across from the KANB.

_____

c. The RAPK is between the FACÉ and the LAML.

_____

LESSON 4

Look at the map and read the sentences. Write **T** (true) or **F** (false). Correct the false sentences.

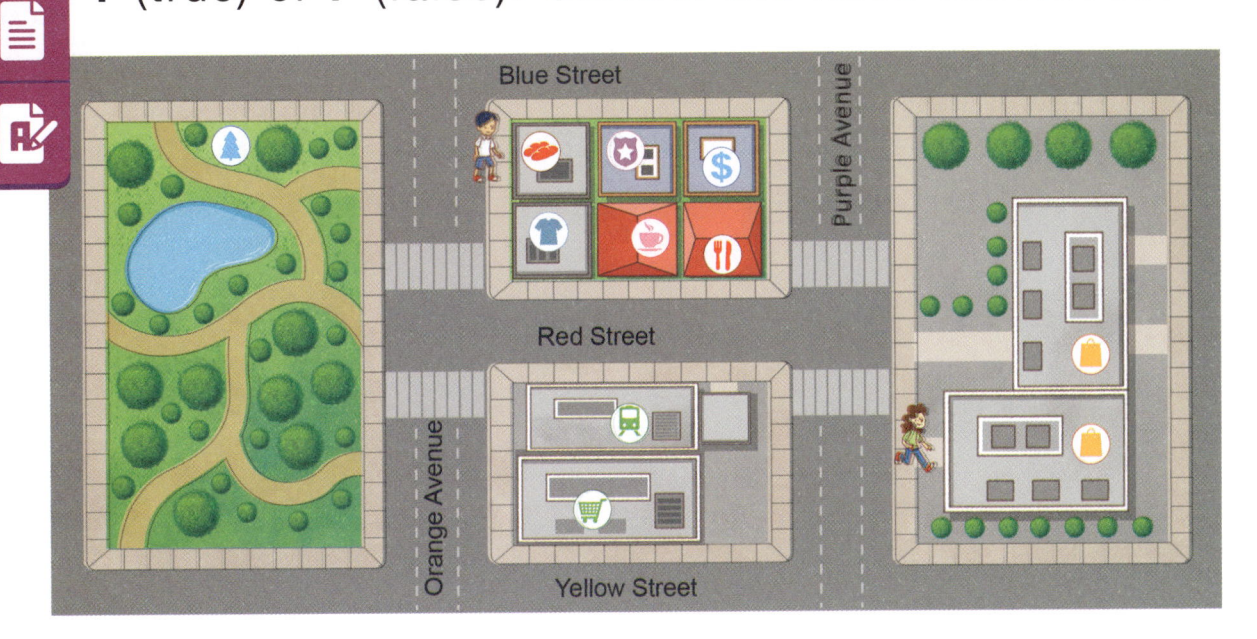

a. The subway station is next to the store.
_____

b. The boy is in front of the bakery.
_____

c. The café is across from the subway station.
_____

d. The police station is between the restaurant and the store.
_____

e. The bank is between the bakery and the café.
_____

f. The girl is in front of the café.
_____

107

WORKBOOK

UNIT 8 — LESSON 1

Complete the missing letters and match the words with the pictures.

a. ch__c__l__t__   c__k__

b. c__ff__ __   w__th   m__lk

c. __r__ng__   j__ __c__

d. ch__c__l__t__   c__ __k__ __

e. h__m   __nd   ch__ __s__   s__ndw__ch

f. str__wb__rr__   p__ __

g. br__ __d   __nd   b__tt__r

h. __gg   s__l__d

LESSON 2

Write the sentences in the speech bubbles.

> An orange juice and a cheese sandwich for me, please.
> A coffee and a strawberry pie for me, please.
> A watermelon juice and a ham and cheese sandwich for me, please.
> A coffee with milk and bread and butter, please.

a. _____

b. _____

c. _____

d. _____

LESSON 3

Circle the appropriate word and draw a picture.

a. A **chocolate** / **orange** cake, please.

b. An **cheese** / **egg** sandwich for me, please.

c. An **orange** / **strawberry** cake, please.

d. An **tangerine** / **apple** juice for me, please.

e. A **cheese** / **egg** sandwich, please.

f. A **orange** / **strawberry** pie.

LESSON 4

Look at the picture and write the orders.

POP CAFÉ MENU
DELICIOUS AND HEALTHY MEALS FOR KIDS

Salads
Green salad
Ceasar salad
$3.99

Snacks
Ham and cheese sandwich
Egg salad sandwich
Bread and butter
$4.99

Desserts
Orange Cake
Chocolate Pie
Strawberry Pie
$1.99

Fruits
Apple
Watermelon
$2.99

Drinks
Juice (Orange or Tangerine)
Coffee
Milk
Hot Chocolate
Water
$1.99

Hello! Welcome to POP Café. May I help you?

BOOK INSTRUCTIONS

Are the sentences right or wrong?
As sentenças estão certas ou erradas?

Ask your classmates' last names.
Pergunte os sobrenomes de seus colegas.

Check the correct option.
Marque a opção correta.

Circle the best alternative.
Circule a melhor alternativa.

Complete the text with the words from the box.
Complete o texto com as palavras do quadro.

Complete using *have* or *has*.
Complete usando *have* ou *has*.

Do the crossword puzzle.
Faça a cruzadinha.

Listen to check your work.
Ouça para conferir seu trabalho.

Listen to the conversation and stick.
Ouça a conversa e cole.

Look at the pictures and answer the questions.
Observe as figuras e responda às perguntas.

Read and draw the places on the map.
Leia e desenhe os lugares no mapa.

Find the answers in the word search.
Encontre as respostas no diagrama.

Unscramble the words.
Desembaralhe as palavras.

Write TRUE or FALSE. Correct the false sentences.
Escreva VERDADEIRO ou FALSO. Corrija as sentenças falsas.

STICKERS

UNIT 1	A,B,C ...

LESSON 2

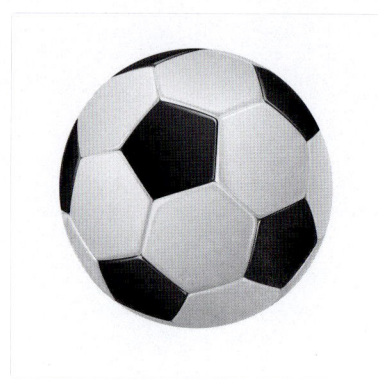

UNIT 2	FAMILY PICTURE

LESSON 2

aunt	brother	grandpa
uncle	brother	grandma
cousin	cousin	dad
grandpa	grandma	mom

114

UNIT 4 **WILD ANIMALS**

LESSON 1

UNIT 5 HOW MANY?
LESSON 2

UNIT 6 MY ROUTINE
LESSON 2

FRI SAT

TUE

THU

WED

SUN

MON

118

UNIT 7 PLACES AROUND
LESSON 3

UNIT 8 YUMMY!
LESSON 3

119